Read & Write

READ & WRITE

Fun Literature and Writing Connections for Kids

Michelle O'Brien-Palmer

illustrations by
Heidi Stephens

MicNik Publications, Inc.

Credits

Illustrations: Heidi Stephens
Cover Art: Denny Driver
Educational Consultant: Lori Blevins Gonwick
Cover Photography: Lance O. Kenyon
Copy Editor: Lory Hess
Content Editors:
Suzie Fiebig, Teacher, Christa McAuliffe Elementary, Lake Washington Schools, Redmond, WA
Suzie Fiebig's 2nd-grade students
Carol Fletcher, Teacher, Carl Sandburg Elementary, Lake Washington Schools, Kirkland, WA
Carol Fletcher's 3rd-grade students
Eileen Gibbons, Teacher, Rochester, NY
Lori Blevins Gonwick, Teacher, Carl Sandburg Elementary, Lake Washington Schools, Kirkland, WA
Lori Blevins Gonwick's 4th-grade students
Martha Ivy's 4th-grade students, Christa McAuliffe Elementary, Lake Washington Schools, Redmond, WA
Marci Larsen, Principal, North Bend, WA
Valerie Marshall's 4th-grade students, Christa McAuliffe Elementary, Lake Washington Schools, Redmond, WA
Julie Neupert's 6th-grade students
Ruby Pannoni, Communication Supervisor, Boyertown Area School District, Bowertown, PA
Mary Schneider, Teacher, Woodinville Montessori, Woodinville, WA
Mary Schneider's 1st and 2nd-grade students
Dr. Katherine Schlick Noe, Professor, Seattle University, Seattle, WA
Joyce Standing, Teacher, The Overlake School, Redmond, WA
Joyce Standing's 5th-grade students

Young Authors:

Erica Reiling, Kindergartener
Danny McCarthy, Kindergartener
Renee-Chantal Arnold, 1st-grader
Yufanyi Nshom, 2nd-grader

Steven Yoo, 3rd-grader
Terry Yoo, 3rd-grader
Nick Palmer, 4th-grader
Brian Schnierer, 4th-grader

Hope Christensen, 4th-grader
Annie Short, 5th-grader
Philip Sanchez, 5th-grader
Juleah Swanson, 6th-grader

ISBN 1-879235-04-8
Library of Congress Catalog Card Number: 94-76002
Copyright © 1994 Michelle O'Brien-Palmer

Manufactured in the United States of America

10 9 8 7 6 5 4 3 2 1

ATTENTION: SCHOOLS AND BUSINESSES

Books from MicNik Publications, Inc., are available at quantity discounts with bulk purchase
for educational, business, or sales promotional use. For information, please write to:
MicNik Publications, Inc.
P.O. Box 3041, Kirkland, WA 98083
(206) 881-6476

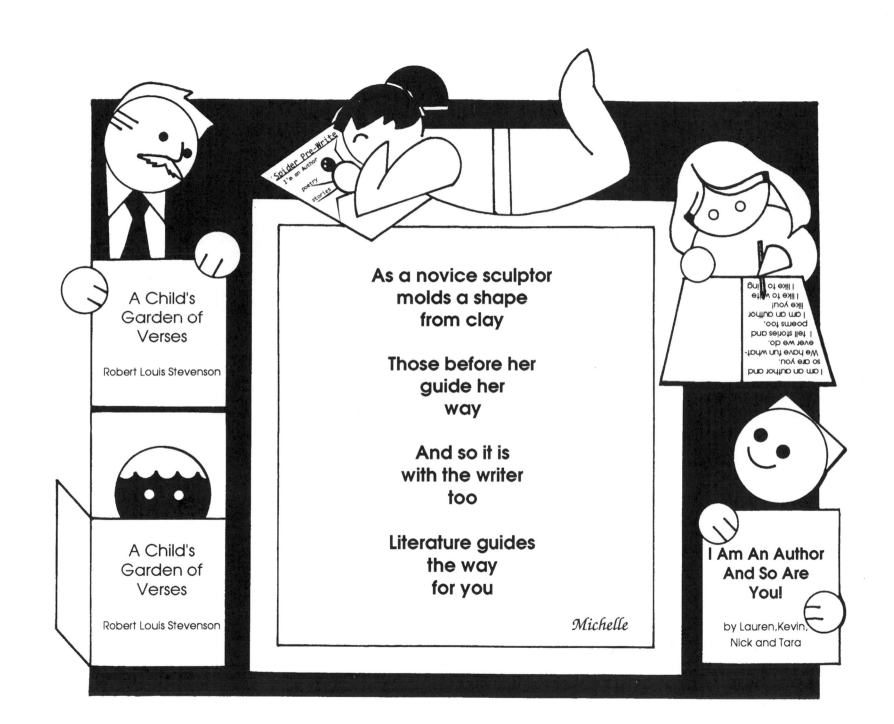

Acknowledgements

I would like to thank the following people for their support and contributions in the creation of *Read & Write*.

I am especially grateful to the children who tested, edited and provided project recommendations, quotes and inspiration for *Read & Write*. You helped to mold and shape *Read & Write* into its final form.

- Thanks to Mary Schneider's first- and second-graders for your great ideas and page examples. I had such fun writing alliteration and stories with you.
- Thanks to Suzie Fiebig's second-graders for sharing your books and projects with me. I really enjoyed watching you create your dioramas and listening to your book-talks!
- Thanks to Carol Fletcher's third-graders for contributing your t-shirt project idea and page examples. It was fun to be a part of your literature circle and discussion times.
- Thanks to Lori Blevins Gonwick's fourth-graders for testing forms, great group feedback, and all of your page examples. I'll always remember your play and handbook discussion.
- Thanks to Valerie Marshall and Martha Ivy's fourth-graders for sharing your weekly literature circles and writing circles along with your book ideas and examples. You taught me so much!
- Thanks to Joyce Standing's fifth-graders for helpful editing comments and page examples. I thoroughly enjoyed your projects and wonderful discussions.
- A special thanks to Julie Neupert's sixth-graders for your weekly editing sessions. Your Chara-a-Graph ideas were wonderful and your editorial comments and suggestions significantly affected *Read & Write*. You are truly great editors!

I also extend sincere thanks to those who helped in the production of this book:

To the young authors for their examples of how to fill out the various forms and their actual projects – Erica Reiling, Dan McCarthy, Renee-Chantal Arnold, Yufanyi Nshom, Terry Yoo, Steven Yoo, Hope Christensen, Nick Palmer, Brian Schnierer, Philip Sanchez, Annie Short, and Juleah Swanson.

To the content editors for their dedication and enriching contributions to this book – Suzie Fiebig, Eileen Gibbons, Marci Larsen, Ruby Pannoni, Dr. Katherine Schlick Noe, Mary Schneider and Joyce Standing.

To Lori Blevins Gonwick for her support and great ideas as the educational consultant, to Heidi Stephens for her wonderful illustrations, to Lory Hess for her professional editing, and to Lance O. Kenyon for his cover photograph.

Thank you Gid and Nick. This book would not have been written without your love and support.

Mary Schneider's 1st/2nd-Grade Class

Michael Abraldes
Austin Brawner
Charlotte Bouscaren
Nicholas Chou
Jared Cohen
Seth Cohen
Shawn Connolly
Rachael Dorman
Logan Gaylord
Jeffrey Hallenbeck
Tony Harmon
Emily Hu
Nic LaPonte
Melissa Lewis
Michael Liang
Amy Locke
Lindsay Marcil
Tyler Matthews
Vijaytha Rathnam
Desi Rawls
Alex Straughan
Jonathon Terpstra
Kate Thueringer
Stephanie Torpy
Wesley Vieira
Nina Wallace

Young Authors

Renee-Chantal Arnold
Hope Christensen
Danny McCarthy
Yufanyi Nshom
Nick Palmer
Erica Reiling
Philip Sanchez
Brian Schnierer
Annie Short
Juleah Swanson
Steven Yoo
Terry Yoo

Valerie Marshall's, Martha Ivy's and Susan Harper's 4th-Grade Class

Micah Barrett
Jamie Bastine
Katie Benson
Blake Blair
Chris Bohner
Eric Brickley
Rory Callahan
Travis Calhoun
Bryan Case
Derek Clopton
Brent Cramer
Michael Cundy
Megan Davis
Michelle Dias
Jonathan Diggs
Ian Farmer
Elizabeth Ferguson
Ryan Focht
Nicole Fuhrman
Janice Fyffe
Matt Garrett
Kelli Hathaway
Chris Hlavaty
Travis Holland
Hayley Hubert
Katie Hulsey
Jessica Humes
Rachel Hutfless
Stephanie Lawson
Jenilee Leadbetter
Kevi Louis-Johnson
Michael Mains
Katie Mathis
Dan Matthias
Jennifer McCormick
Melissa Murray
Alicia Nason
Tyler Norton
Elisabeth Olson
Dustin Owen
David Pierce
Marcie Peterson
Katie Quigley
Garrett Quinn
Jonathan Rayment
Van Riley
Makell Rons
Marcella Rosanova
Matt Schwagler
Chris Sepanski
Allison Serrano
Shelby Severin
Kyle VanWinkle
George Vigeland
Ryan Wallace
Kevin Watt
Erin Zambroski

Suzie Fiebig's 2nd-Grade Class

Lindsey Baggette
Billy Botner
Margaret Bruya
Anthony Cao
Lindsay Carr
Joelle Cramer
Landon Davis
Katherine Diggs
William Dodd
Thomas Edwards
Christopher Fowler
Christy Harrison
Brian Hebert
Christine Heckeroth
Matthew Holtmeier
Ariel Jordan
Jessica Kosak
Sarah Lawson
Ian Mathews
Elizabeth McKay
Roger Newman
Yufanyi Nshom
Kelsey Peronto
Stephen Sanoja
Stimson Snead
John Velazquez
Hali Walther

Quotes by Others

Emily Gibbons
Hannah Gibbons
Megan Gibbons
Tara O'Brien
Allison Palmer
Matt Palmer
Steven Reiling
Gavin Schroeder
Michelle Short
Carly White

Lori Blevins Gonwick's 4th-Grade Class

Weston Bearwood
Taylor Blanchard
Nicole Brazee
Hope Christensen
Briett Easterlin
Kim Egan
Tracy Faulds
Katie Ferguson
Kenyon Ferris
Greg Frost
James Gilleland
Hailey Heinrich
Jason Hermann
Kelsey Jacobson
Amy Johnston
Kobie Krogh
Paul Lee
Tim Lucia
Ryan Major
Stephanie McAuley
Perry Nelson
Lily Passavant
Jamie Rosvall
Derek Smith
Vashti Tate
Jessica Walsh

Joyce Standing's 5th-Grade Class

Michael Armstrong
Kai Corby
Lindi Duesenberg
Dan Fairbanks
Carie Fowler
Sabrina Hirsch
Jonathan Lin
Cara McEvoy
Megan Meyers
Alex Pickrell
Gareth Reece
Jordan Sherwood-Hill
Rachel Vaskevitch
C.P. Waite
David Waldbaum
Stephanie Wei

Julee Neupert's 6th-Grade Class

B.J. Arnold
Divine Aquino
Patrick Atherton
Sean Bell
Jessica Bleeker
John Eitel
Dewey Halpaus
Heather Holt
Carly Jasperson
Brad LeVeck
Matt LeVeck
Kristan Locke
Jeff Lyons
Theresa Mangahas
Mark McIntosh
Kierstin Stettler

Carol Fletcher's 3rd-Grade Class

Jason Abdo
Allen Adair
Brandon Alborg
Harrison Bishop
Rebecca Blackman
Nicholas Caluori
Kristen Dunseth-Orth
Tarisha Gregory
Sarah Hale
Miranda Haworth
Derek Head
Geneva Hurst
Jared McCarton
BJ Neil
Dani Newby
Kallen Paddock
Roya Salahshoor
Kim Simmons
Allison Stites
Matt Stuhring
Kirk Thorson
Brandon Winslow
Nicholas Xidias
Jessica Zigweid

Table of Contents

Introduction
for parents and teachers

READ & WRITE: Fun Literature and Writing Connections for Kids is written to help children (K-6th grade) identify core literary concepts such as character development, setting development, and plot development in the books they read and then integrate what they've learned into their own writing. This text is the third in a whole language series, which includes *Book-Write: A Creative Bookmaking Guide for Young Authors* and *Book-Talk: Exciting Literature Experiences for Kids*. It assumes that the reader is familiar with the five step writing process: pre-writing, drafting, revision, editing, and final copy. Chapter 8: Reference Books lists *Book-Write* and other titles which will be helpful in guiding young authors through the writing process.

At first glance *Read & Write* seems to emphasize reading more than writing. However, every experience in this book was chosen with a writing connection in mind. Analysis of other authors' work helps the young author to integrate new literary concepts into her own writing. Just as the artist learns to fine-tune her skills by modeling artistic styles, the author learns to fine-tune her skills by modeling other authors' styles. Through this practice we all find our own personal style.

Although the text speaks to children directly, it will require adult supervision and guidance in most cases. Many chapters include a page defining the main topic and a page giving information about the chapter's contents. Whenever more information might be helpful to parents or teachers it will be found in italics just under the top border of a text page. The second chapter (Story Style) includes a starter list of books recommended by *Read & Write* teachers. The titles listed are books which model certain literary concepts in a very basic or exaggerated way. It is meant to be a spring-board as you identify many more resources from your own library. There is also a chapter of forms for you to use with your readers and writers at home or school. Make as many copies of these forms as you need. The resource chapter at the end of the book is intended to provide a list of excellent references for bringing literature and the writing process into the home or classroom.

Each idea in this book is meant to be taken as liberally as possible. There is no one right way to do anything. The more variations created, the more exciting the process will be.

Foreword
Note to Kids

I really enjoy reading books and I also learn a lot about writing from the books I read. For instance, I notice the patterns and the words that other authors use in their writing. As I've learned more and more about the tools used by other authors, I've learned to identify and use these tools in my own writing.

I visit many different classrooms and talk with kids every day about the books they read and the stories they write. We have a lot in common. It seems that they too are learning about writing from the books they read. I invited the kids in seven classrooms (1st grade – 6th grade) and twelve young authors (K – 6th grade) to help me write this book. They tested and approved each page. The classrooms and young authors have shared their examples of how the authors of their favorite books create characters, setting and plot. They also show how to use some of the tools used by other authors, like alliteration and story patterns. In Chapter 6: Projects Recommended by Kids, you will find fun reading and writing projects which come highly recommended by the kids involved in this book.

Have fun reading and writing!

Chapter 1

Introduction

Introduction to Read & Write:
Fun Literature and Writing Connections for Kids

This chapter provides a brief introduction to each main chapter. For more detailed information please see the actual chapter. *READ & WRITE* was written with the help of over 200 kids. They were part of the writing and editing process. The young authors who share their unedited examples of forms and projects in the book are listed below:

Erica Reiling	Kindergarten student
Danny McCarthy	Kindergarten student
Renee-Chantal Arnold	1st- grade student
Yufanyi Nshom	2nd-grade student
Terry Yoo	3rd-grade student
Stephen Yoo	3rd-grade student
Nick Palmer	4th-grade student
Brian Schnierer	4th-grade student
Hope Christensen	4th-grade student
Philip Sanchez	5th-grade student
Annie Short	5th-grade student
Juleah Swanson	6th-grade student

Chapter 2: Story Style

In this chapter readers will have an opportunity to explore the words, tools and patterns used by their favorite authors. Readers will be introduced to special literary terms in The Language of Authors Glossary. They will be able to select books using the Book Advice Guide and can use the Starter List to help identify books which model different writing styles. Many different facets of writing are featured, including alliteration, story patterns, graphing the intensity of various events in a story and a special tool box to identify the imagery, similes, metaphors and hyberbole used by other authors.

Chapter 3: Story Setting

Authors describe story settings in many different ways. This chapter suggests a number of ways to view the setting of a story. Readers can evaluate how realistic a story's setting seems to them and identify the setting mood(s) in the Setting Check Sheet. Projects include describing setting in a fun poem, drawing the setting on a stage, creating trading cards of story settings, and re-writing a story using another setting.

Chapter 4: Story Characters

In this chapter readers will explore character development. The Character Profile asks the reader to look at the world through the eyes of a book character. The Sensational Sociogram diagrams the relationships between characters in a story. The reader can evaluate the realism of story characters and identify character traits using the Character Check Sheet.

Chapter 5: Story Plot

Authors use different techniques to create exciting storylines. The goal is to keep the reader interested in the story. This chapter uses a Film strip Story Sequencer and Story Comic Strip to identify the sequence of events in a story. The Problem & Solution Diagram example shows how to think through the problems and solutions presented by the author. Once the key events in a story are identified, the author's plot strategy can be revealed by graphing the conflict, climax and resolution on the Graph-a-Plot.

Chapter 6: Projects Recommended by Kids

Kids can design their own t-shirt around a character from a story they've written or write a story monologue to share with their friends. This chapter is full of fun reading and writing projects recommended by the 200 kids involved in the creation of *Read & Write*. As the classrooms and young authors share their favorite projects with you, think about your own favorite projects and share them with your friends. Once you've decided which project to do first, you will find a Project Sheet at the back of the chapter to help you get organized.

Chapter 2

Story Style

Story Style

"I like it when an author makes it very exciting and you won't know what happens if you don't finish the book." Steven Reiling, 3rd grade

Style refers to the unique way each author tells a story. The patterns and language chosen by an author in the creation of a story represent his or her style of writing.

In this chapter you will have an opportunity to explore the words, tools, and patterns used by your favorite authors. The Language of Authors Glossary defines some common words used by writers. Select the type of book and difficulty level you would like to read using BAG IT: Book Advice Guide. The Pattern Quilt is a fun way to create stories based upon a book you've read. Try creating a poem or story using alliteration.

As you experiment with the style tools presented in this chapter, you will begin to create your personal writing style.

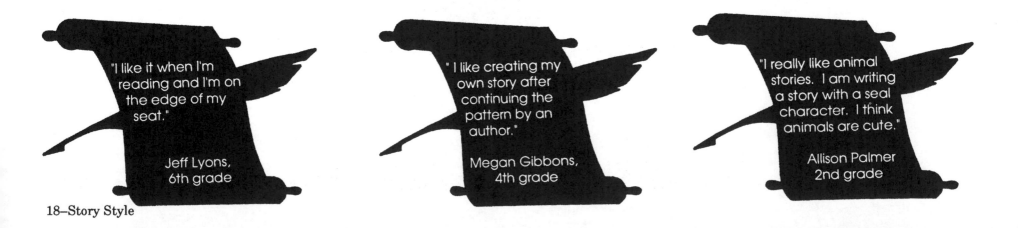

"I like it when I'm reading and I'm on the edge of my seat."

Jeff Lyons,
6th grade

" I like creating my own story after continuing the pattern by an author."

Megan Gibbons,
4th grade

"I really like animal stories. I am writing a story with a seal character. I think animals are cute."

Allison Palmer
2nd grade

About This Chapter

This chapter includes...

Story Style: Explore many dimensions of story style through...

The writing connections in each activity will help you use what you are learning about story style in your own writing.

The Language of Authors Glossary

Acrostic Poem A type of poem which uses each letter in the name of a noun to write a description (see page 47).

All-Knowing Point of View The author tells the story from the outside telling everything all of the characters do, feel and think.

Allegory A story or poem which teaches a moral or lesson through its characters and plot.

Alliteration The repetition of the same beginning sound in two or more words (see page 29).

Characters The people or animals who are part of the story. See Chapter 4.

Conflict The problems in a story. There are four types of conflict used in stories. They are character against character, nature, herself/himself, and society (see page 103).

Climax The peak of the conflict in a story. The climax comes just before the conflict is resolved (see diagram on page 103).

Date line Tells what city and state a news story came from and when the story was written.

Dialogue Conversation between characters.

Draft An unfinished piece of writing. The second step in the writing process; pre-write, draft, revise, edit, and final copy.

Edit To check a piece of writing for any spelling, punctuation and grammatical changes. Fourth step in the writing process.

Fiction Imaginary stories. They come from the imagination of the author.

Figurative Language Describing something by comparing it to something else. Figurative language includes similes, and metaphors (see examples on page 37).

First Person The author becomes a character telling the story. Readers often feel as if they are the "I" character in a story written from the first person point of view.

Flat Character A character who does not grow and change in a story (see page 77).

The Language of Authors Glossary

Genre The type of story. The categories can include poetry, mystery, and many others (see page 24).

Headline Gives just enough information in a news story to attract the reader to the story (see page 25).

Hyperbole Exaggeration used for emphasis in a story. It is sometimes used to create humor (see page 37).

Imagery The author uses words that appeal to the senses in creating the story (see page 37).

Metaphor A comparison between two unlike things suggesting that they are similar.

Mood The feelings you get when you are reading a story (see the mood list on page 55).

Non fiction True stories and informational books based upon facts.

Personification Giving human characteristics and traits to non-humans.

Plot The structure of a story. It includes characters, setting, problems, climax, and resolution (page 103).

Point of View The perspective used to tell a story: all knowing, first person, or third person.

Pre-Write The first step in the writing process. Pre-writing helps you to create writing ideas.

Resolution The problem in a story is solved.

Revision Checking to see if your story says what you want it to say. The third step of the writing process.

Round Character A character who changes and grows in a story.

Setting Where and when the story takes place. See Chapter 3.

Simile Comparison linking two unlike things using the word "like" or "as."

Style The special way an author uses language and patterns to tell his/her story.

Theme The main message in a story. It is the lesson or the main idea.

Third Person The author tells the story from the outside. Only what is seen and heard is reported.

Read & Write Starter List

Reading and Writing Strategies Demonstrated in Literature Recommended by *Read & Write* Teachers, Lori Blevins Gonwick and Suzanne Fiebig

Title	Author
Alliteration:	
(Use to model alliteration and the format for ABC books)	
A My Name Is Alice	Bayer
The Z was Zapped	Van Allsburg
Zoophabets	Talon
Cause/Effect:	
(Use to identify if/then relationships and predict events.)	
Fortunately	Charlip
If You Give a Mouse a Cookie	Numeroff
If You Give a Mouse A Muffin	Numeroff
That's Good, That's Bad	Cuyler
The Little House	Burton
Runaway Bunny	Brown
Character Traits:	
(Use to identify obvious character traits)	
Little Red Riding Hood	Marshall
The Three Little Pigs	Bishop
The Hundred Dresses	Estes
Compare/Contrast (Variations):	
(Use to encourage children to re-tell stories and create their own folktales/fairytales)	
Jim and the Beanstalk	Briggs
Lon Po Po	Young
Prince Cinders	Cole
The Principal's New Clothes	Calmenson
Sleeping Ugly	Yolen
Snow White in New York	French

Title	Author
Descriptive Language/Adjectives:	
(Use to demonstrate descriptive language)	
Aurora Means Dawn	Sanders
Guess Who My Favorite Person Is?	Baylor
Knots on a Counting Rope	Archambault
Owl Moon	Yolen
Dialogue:	
(Use to show dialogue in a simple, clear, way so students can easily transfer this concept into their own writing)	
Frog and Toad	Lobel
Stella Luna	Cameron
The Day Jimmy's Boa Ate the Wash	Kellogg
Parts of Speech/Style:	
(Use to model style skills/strategies in context)	
A Cache of Jewels (Groupings)	Heller
Chocolate Moose for Dinner (Homonyms)	Gwyne
I Love You, Goodnight (Similes)	Buller
Little Fish, Big Fish (Nouns/Verbs)	Asch
Many Lucious Lollipops (Adjectives)	Heller
Odds and Ends Alvy (Classification)	Frank
The Hungry Thing (Rhyming)	Seidler
The Hungry Thing Returns (Rhyming)	Seider
The King Who Rained (Homonyms)	Gwyne
The Pagemaster (Adjectives)	Kirschner/ Contreras

Read & Write Starter List
(Continued)

Title	Author
Plot (Conflict/Resolution):	
(Use to model conflict, resolution and story structure)	
Arthur's Teacher Trouble	Brown
Jack and the Beanstalk	Kellogg
Jacob Two-Two Meets the Hooded Fang	Richler
Just a Dream	Van Allsburg
Leo the Late Bloomer	Kraus
Mufaro's Beautiful Daughters	Steptoe
My Grandma has Black Hair	Hoffman
The Grouchy Ladybug	Carle
The Pain and the Great One	Blume

Title	Author
Plot (Surprise):	
(Use to show exciting and surprise endings. They are great motivators for student writers)	
Imogene's Antlers	Small
Jumanji	Van Allsburg
The Emperor's New Clothes	Wescott
The Polar Express	Van Allsburg
The Principal's New Clothes	Calmenson

Title	Author
Repetition/Rhyme:	
(Use to inspire young poets and model story patterning)	
Chicka Chicka Boom Boom	Martin Jr.
Hairy Bear	Wright Group
"I Can't" Said the Ant	Cameron
The Very Busy Spider	Carle
The Very Hungry Caterpillar	Carle
I Know an Old Lady Who Swallowed a Fly	Westcott

Title	Author
Sequels:	
(Use books and sequels to model extending stories. They are great for predicting what will happen next and how characters will behave)	
Cat Wings – Cat Wings Return	LeGuin
My Father's Dragon –	
Elmer and the Dragon –	
The Dragons of Blueland	Gannett
Tales of a Fourth Grade Nothing –	
Super Fudge –	
Fudgemania	Blume
The Hungry Thing –	
The Hungry Thing Returns	Seidler
The Indian in the Cupboard –	
The Return of the Indian –	
The Secret of the Indian –	
The Mystery of the Cupboard	Banks

Title	Author
Sequencing:	
(Use to show the logical sequence of events and story progression)	
Stringbean's Trip to the Shining Sea	Williams
The Mitten	Brett
Three Bears	Brett
Three Little Pigs	Marshall

BAG IT: Book Advice Guide

Lori Blevins Gonwick's BAG IT idea helps her fourth-grade students to select a book considering genre (through color coded dots) and level of difficulty. Each child is given a BAG IT bag to use with the class-room library. All books are categorized by genre dots and difficulty levels (see illustration below).

Materials:
Paper bag (copy – page 136)
Markers
Labeled books and bins   Symbols (page 136)

Goals:
To select books to read
To explore different types (genres) of books

Steps:
1. Copy the BAG IT form on page 136.
2. Color in the circles on the form to match the color code on the next page.
3. Paste the form onto a lunch bag.
4. Use your paper bag "BAG IT" to decide the type of book (genre) you want to read.
5. Decide the level of difficulty for your book.
6. Check your classroom library for the color-coded bin with the genre you've chosen.
7. Find the difficulty level you've selected.

Book Advice Guide Example

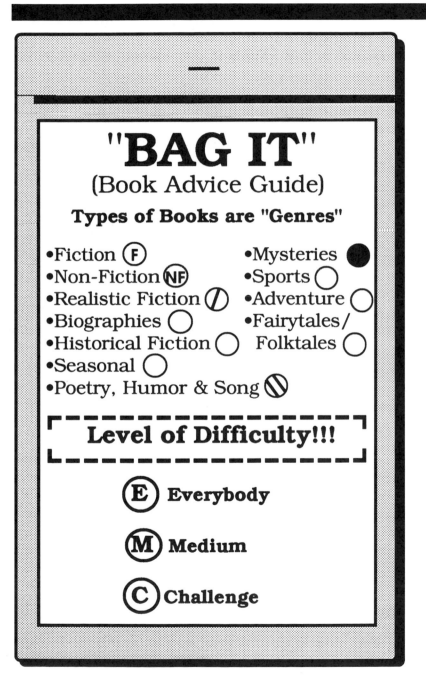

Types of Books are "Genres"

Dot Color	Genre	Definition	Symbol
F orange	**Fiction**	Imaginary Stories	F
NF green	**Non-Fiction**	True Stories	NF
⊘ orange	**Realistic Fiction**	Stories based on things that could really happen	
○ white	**Biographies**	True stories about real people	
○ brown	**Historical Fiction**	Imaginary stories based on historical events	
○ red	**Seasonal**	Stories based on holidays	
⊘ white	**Poetry, Song & Humor**	Rhymes, songs and funny books	
● black	**Mysteries**	Stories with suspense and problems to solve	
○ yellow	**Sports**	Stories based on different types of sports	
○ purple	**Adventure**	Exciting journeys to interesting places	
○ blue	**Folktales/ Fairytales**	Stories with a moral – good against evil	

The Literature Handbook

Valerie Marshall and Martha Ivy use their handbook idea with the students in their fourth-grade classroom. Lori Blevins Gonwick's fourth graders enjoyed the Literature Handbook so much they used it as a group activity (see class example recorded by Tracy Faulds).

Materials:
White paper (11" x 16 1/2")   Pencil/pen/markers

Goal:
To identify nouns, adjectives and verbs used by other authors

Steps:
1. Create a literature handbook using the directions on page 27.
2. Read a chapter in your book.
3. Re-read the chapter looking for nouns, verbs and adjectives the author uses. Record them on the special pages in your handbook.
4. Use a dictionary if you need help identifying a word as a noun, adjective or verb.

Writing Connection:
Use some of the words and phrases you've recorded in your own stories

The Literature Handbook Example

Step 1 and Step 2

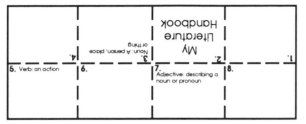

Fold the paper into eight panels.

In panel 2: write "Literature Handbook"
panel 3: write "noun" and definition
panel 5: write "verb" and definition
panel 7: write "adjectives" and definition

Step 3

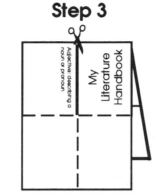

Fold sheet in half length-wise. Cut between panels 2, 7 and 3,6.

Step 4

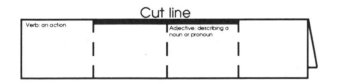

Open the sheet again and fold it in half.

Step 5

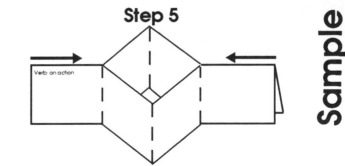

Push the end sections together and it will fold itself.

Step 6

Finished Handbook

My Literature Handbook

Sample Pages

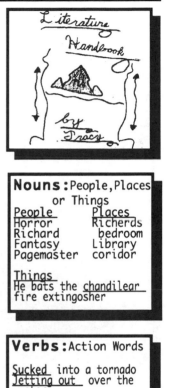

Literature Handbook by Tracy

Nouns: People, Places or Things

People	Places
Horror	Richerds
Richard	bedroom
Fantasy	Library
Pagemaster	coridor

Things
He bats the chandilear
fire extingosher

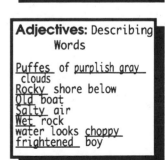

Verbs: Action Words

Sucked into a tornado
Jetting out over the water
Clinging to the cliff
She shrieked
He was quivering
Sliped on a rock
Adventure led the way
sprang up in his bed

Adjectives: Describing Words

Puffes of purplish gray clouds
Rocky shore below
Old boat
Salty air
Wet rock
water looks choppy
frightened boy

Alluring Alliteration

The second-grade students in Mary Schneider's class had a wonderful time creating their own alluring alliterations. They brainstormed the words in the example with help from their dictionaries.

Alger the Alligator

Materials:
Form (copy – page 137)   Pencil

Goals:
To create sentences using alliteration
To practice using a dictionary

Steps:
1. Select the letter you want to use in your sentence.
2. List animals/nouns whose names start with the letter you've chosen (see example).
3. List action words (verbs) which start with the letter (see example).
4. List describing words (adjectives) which start with the letter (see example).
5. Write your sentences using words from your lists.

Writing Connection:
Try using alliteration in the stories you write

Alluring Alliteration Example

Alluring Alliteration

with Alger the Astonishing Alligator

Animal (noun)	Action (verb)	Description (adjective)
dog	demand	dappled
dinosaur	dangerous	deadly
dragon	damaged	delicious
dolphin	dancing	depressed
dove	drumming	diseased
dartmouth	darting	delicate
daddy longlegs	dating	daring
dalmation	defeated	distinguished
dingo	delivered	disguised

"A deadly, dappled dragon demanded the dangerous daddy longlegs drop the delicious dish." *by Nina Wallace and Emily Hu*

Story Pattern Quilt

Mary Schneider's first graders enjoyed identifying story patterns and then creating their own similarly patterned stories.

Story Pattern

___ ___ eats _____
___ ___ eats _____
They love to ___ and ___

Jumpin Jerry eats beets
Merry Mary eats sweets
They love to eat and eat

Happy Harvey eats jam
Pretty Pam eats ham
They love to eat spam

Big Billy eats chicken legs
Nice Nancy eats chicken eggs
They love to eat meat

Picky Nicky eats peas
Terrific Tara eats cheese
They love to eat what
they please

Materials:
Pencil/pen/markers   Paper

Goals:
To identify story patterns
To create your own story from the patterns

Steps:
1. Read a book with repeated words or a pattern.
2. Identify and record the pattern.
3. Use the pattern to create your own story.
4. Take all of the stories and make a quilt.

Writing Connection:
Create your own pattern and use it to write your stories or poems

Story Pattern Quilt Example

| Silly | | went | to | town | doing | | upside | down. |

| | On | the | way | she/he | met | a | | |

| | | They | | | |

from *Silly Sally*
by Audrey Wood

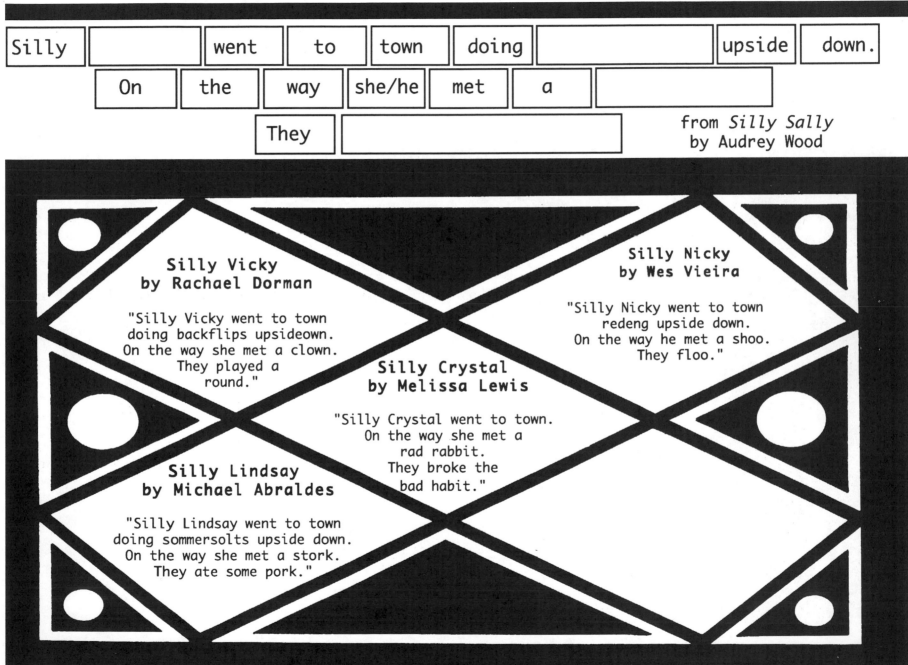

Silly Vicky
by Rachael Dorman

"Silly Vicky went to town
doing backflips upsideown.
On the way she met a clown.
They played a
round."

Silly Nicky
by Wes Vieira

"Silly Nicky went to town
redeng upside down.
On the way he met a shoo.
They floo."

Silly Crystal
by Melissa Lewis

"Silly Crystal went to town.
On the way she met a
rad rabbit.
They broke the
bad habit."

Silly Lindsay
by Michael Abraldes

"Silly Lindsay went to town
doing sommersolts upside down.
On the way she met a stork.
They ate some pork."

Pattern Spider Pre-Write

The Pattern Spider Pre-write is a fun individual, buddy and group activity. It helps students brainstorm ideas for a story of their own or a story based around a theme created by another author.

Materials:
Form (copy – page 138)   Pencil/pen

Goals:
To identify a story pattern
To create your own pre-write from the
 story pattern you identify

Steps:
1. Read a book with a strong pattern.
2. Identify and record the pattern.
3. Use the Pattern Spider Pre-write form to
   create your own pre-write.

Writing Connection:
Follow your pre-write as you write your
 own story

Pattern Spider Pre-Write

This pattern came from *Alexander and the Terrible, Horrible, No Good, Very Bad Day* by Judith Viorst

Name: Steven and Terry

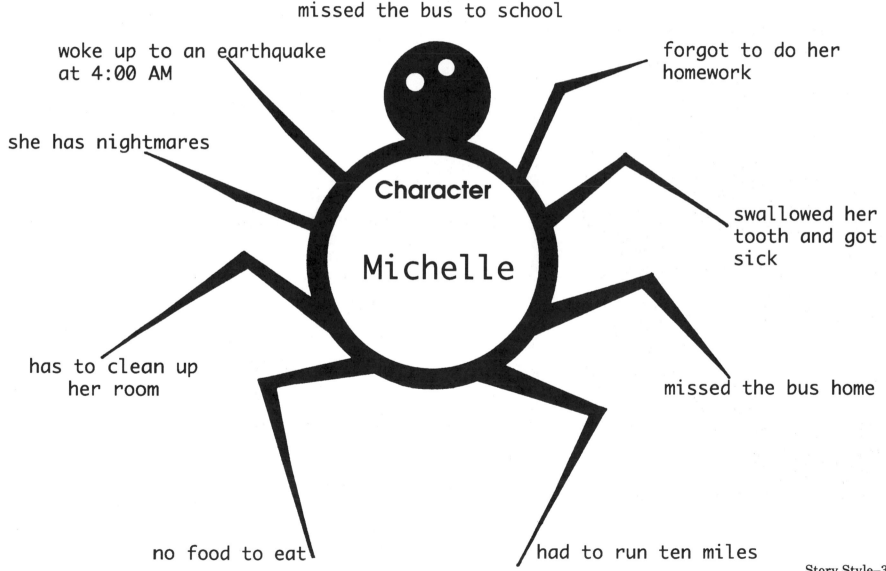

missed the bus to school

woke up to an earthquake
at 4:00 AM

forgot to do her
homework

she has nightmares

Character

Michelle

swallowed her
tooth and got
sick

has to clean up
her room

missed the bus home

no food to eat

had to run ten miles

Bar Graph

T[...] de students worked together to create the Bar Graph example. They u[...] the author of the book they all read kept the interest level high thro[...]

Materials:
Form (copy – page 139)   Pencil/pen

Goal:
To graph the intensity of a story's events

Steps:
1. Read your book.
2. Identify and order the ten main events in the story.
3. Rate the intensity of the events on a scale of 1 to 10 (see example).
4. Graph the events using a bar graph like the one in the example.
5. Note the pattern the author uses to keep the reader's attention.

Writing Connection:
If you feel that the pattern kept your interest, try using it in your stories

Bar Graph Example

by
Alex Pickrell
C.P. Waite
Michael Armstrong

Island of the Blue Dolphins
Event Intensity Graph

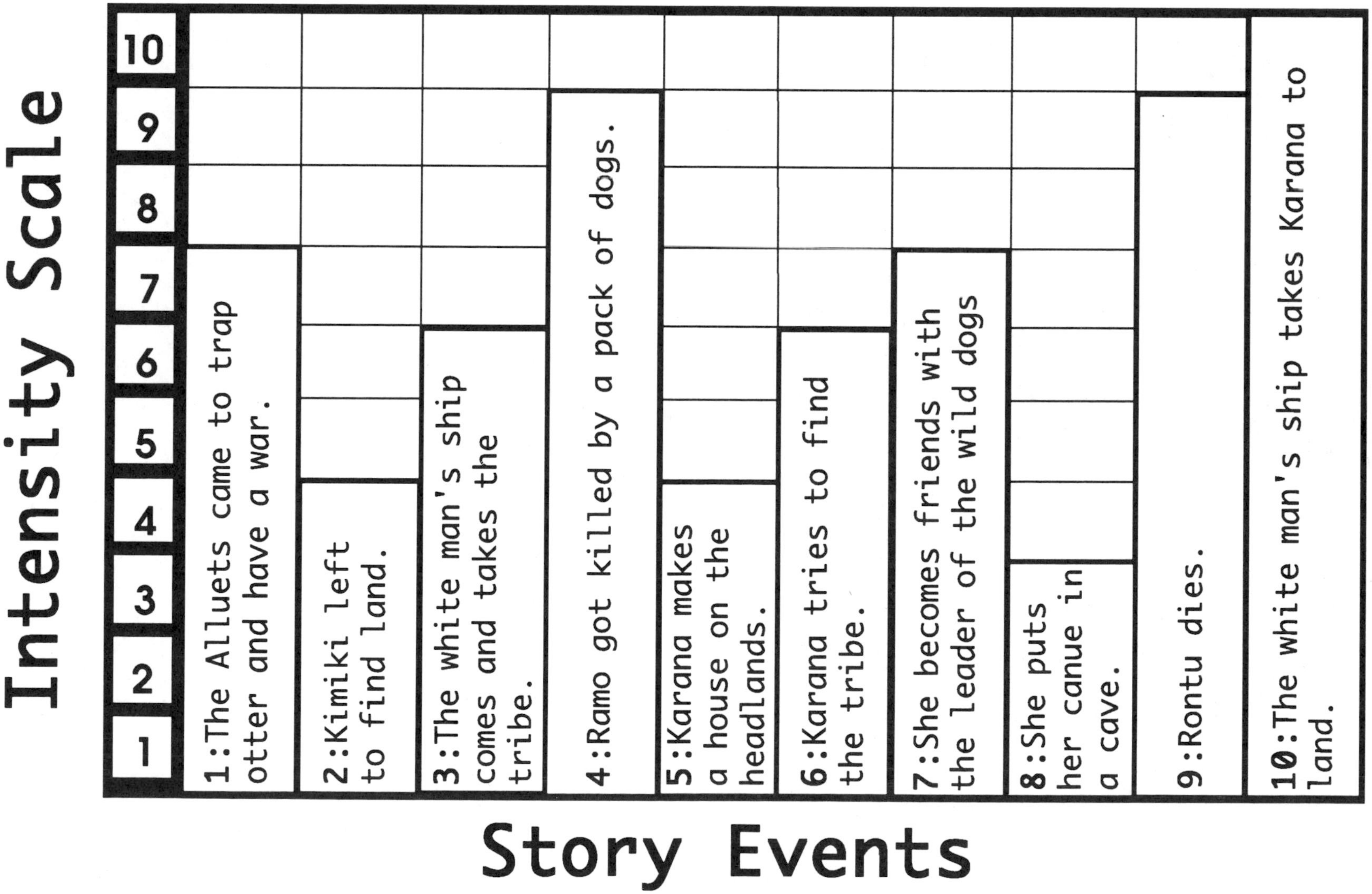

Intensity Scale

| 10 |
| 9 |
| 8 |
| 7 |
| 6 |
| 5 |
| 4 |
| 3 |
| 2 |
| 1 |

1:The Alluets came to trap otter and have a war.

2:Kimiki left to find land.

3:The white man's ship comes and takes the tribe.

4:Ramo got killed by a pack of dogs.

5:Karana makes a house on the headlands.

6:Karana tries to find the tribe.

7:She becomes friends with the leader of the wild dogs

8:She puts her canue in a cave.

9:Rontu dies.

10:The white man's ship takes Karana to land.

Story Events

Style Tool Box

The Style Tool Box is intended for older students. This is meant to be a challenging activity. Teachers find that an introductory lesson on similes, metaphors, imagery, and hyperbole is necessary. It is a fun group or partner activity.

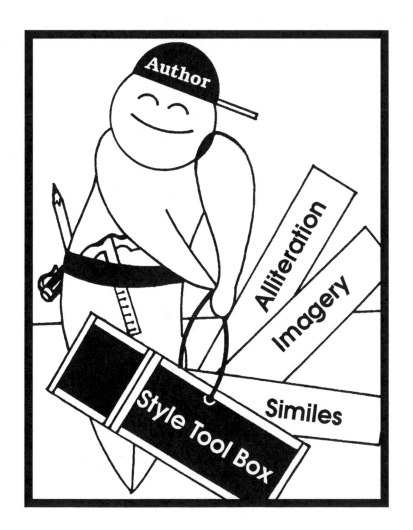

Materials:
Form (copy – page 140)   Pencil/pen

Goal:
To record examples of imagery, similes, metaphors and hyperbole used by authors

Steps:
1. Read a chapter in your book.
2. Think about the pictures the words painted in your mind.
3. Re-read the chapter recording some of the similes, metaphors, hyperbole and imagery used by the author.
4. Look at books by other authors. Note the style tools used most often by each author.

Writing Connection:
Try using some of the tools in the style tool box in your own story

Style Tool Box Example

Name: Juleah and Nick

AUTHOR TOOLS

"clear moonlit night"
"the square brick building"
"watery blue eyes"
from *Danny The Champion of the World* by Roald Dahl

"The barn was very large. It was very old. It smelled of hay and it smelled of manure."
from *Charlotte's Web* by E.B. White

IMAGERY: Appeals to the senses

"frail as a soap bubble"
"eyes felt like cotton balls"
"face lit up as if he had just won the lottery"
"pale as a new moon"

from *Sisters Long Ago* by Peg Kehret

SIMILES: Comparison between unlike things using like or as

"a fair is a rat's paradise"
"you will find a veritable treasure of popcorn..."
"a rotten egg is a regular stink bomb"
from *Charlotte's Web* by E.B. White

METAPHORS: Comparisons suggesting things are similar

"I will die of a broken heart" from *Charlotte's Web* by E.B. White

"stormed out of the room"
from *Sisters Long Ago* by Peg Kehret

HYPERBOLE: Exaggeration used to make a point

Point of View Journal

Older students find point of view an interesting concept. They like to compare and contrast different points of view. The first person point of view easily lends itself to writing fun by changing the character telling the story.

Materials:

Paper   Pencil/pen

Goals:

To identify the story point of view
To evaluate the effect of the point of view

Steps:

1. Select the story you want to use.
2. Think about the point of view in the story you've selected.
3. Write your thoughts in your journal.
4. If you would like ideas for your journal you can use the topics listed.

Writing Connection:

Try writing stories from different points of view and evaluate how it changes the story

Point of View Journal Example

Possible Journal Topics

- From what point of view was the story written?
- What other stories have you read that are written from this point of view?
- Do you think the author made a good decision in writing from this point of view? Why?
- How would the story change if it were told by someone else?
- Re-write the story using a different point of view.

Point of View

All knowing point of view:
The author tells the story from the outside and tells what the characters do, feel and think.

First Person:
The author becomes a character telling the story.

Third Person:
The author tells the story from the outside and reports what is seen and heard.

Nick
March 17, 1994
Book: *The Return of the Indian*

    The Return of the Indian is written in the third person. Most of the books I read are told by characters. Like the scientist tells his story in *The Time Machine*. *Castle in the Attic* is told by William.

    I agree with using the third person in this story because I don't think it would sound very good if it was told by a character. If Patrick told the story there would be a lot missing. Patrick didn't even come into the story until half way through. The whole beginning would be missing.

Chapter 3
Story Setting

Story Setting

The **Setting** is where and when a story takes place. Some settings stay the same throughout the story. Other stories may be set in many different places and many different time periods. The author decides what setting(s) will create just the right background for the story.

When thinking about setting, the author must also determine the mood of the story. In a mystery or adventure, the mood might be suspenseful. In a humorous book, the mood might be silly or playful. The author creates the mood that best fits the story.

In this chapter, you will have an opportunity to identify the setting in a story. You will look at how authors create the setting using their own special language and you will determine whether or not you feel that the author was successful in creating the story setting.

"I like stories that take place in the city, the woods and the mountains!"

Kirk Thorson,
3rd grade

"If the setting seems realistic and you feel like you're there, it's a good book"

Kristan Locke,
6th grade

"I like trees and the Berenstain Bear's tree house. I like the way it looks, all nice and cozy"

Hannah Gibbons,
Kindergarten

About This Chapter

This chapter includes...

The writing connections in each activity will help you use what you are learning about setting in your own writing.

Setting Stage

The Setting Stage is fun for all ages. Younger authors can dictate their setting descriptions. The scrapbook on page 70 can also be used to identify story settings.

Materials:
Form (copy – page 141)   Pencil/pen/markers

Goals:
To identify the story setting
To draw what you think the main story setting
  looks like

Steps:
1. Think about where the story takes place
   (setting) and imagine what it looks like.
2. Draw a picture of the setting inside the
   stage.
3. Write how it looks in words underneath
   your drawing.
4. Share your drawing with your friends
   as you tell them about the setting.

Writing Connection:
Draw a setting you might like to include in
  your own story

Setting Stage Example

Name: Yufanyi
Title: *The Story of the Missing Red Mitten*
Author: Steven Kellogg

Description:
This is *The Story of the Missing Red Mitten* by Steven Kellogg. This picture is the garden where she finds her mitten.

Poetic Scenes

The Poetic Scenes give readers an opportunity to describe settings in drawings and a fun acrostic poem.

Materials:
Paper   Pencil/pen/markers

Goals:
To identify the settings in the story
To describe the settings using poetry

Steps:
1. Think through the story you have read.
2. Select three settings from the story.
3. Draw the story settings in your own clouds.
4. Write the name of each setting place in a line going down the page (see example).
5. Using each letter of the word, describe the setting (see example).

Writing Connection:
Create the setting for your story by thinking of a place you have been and writing a poem describing this place

Poetic Scene Examples

Name: Nick
Author: Gary Paulsen
Title: *Hatchet*

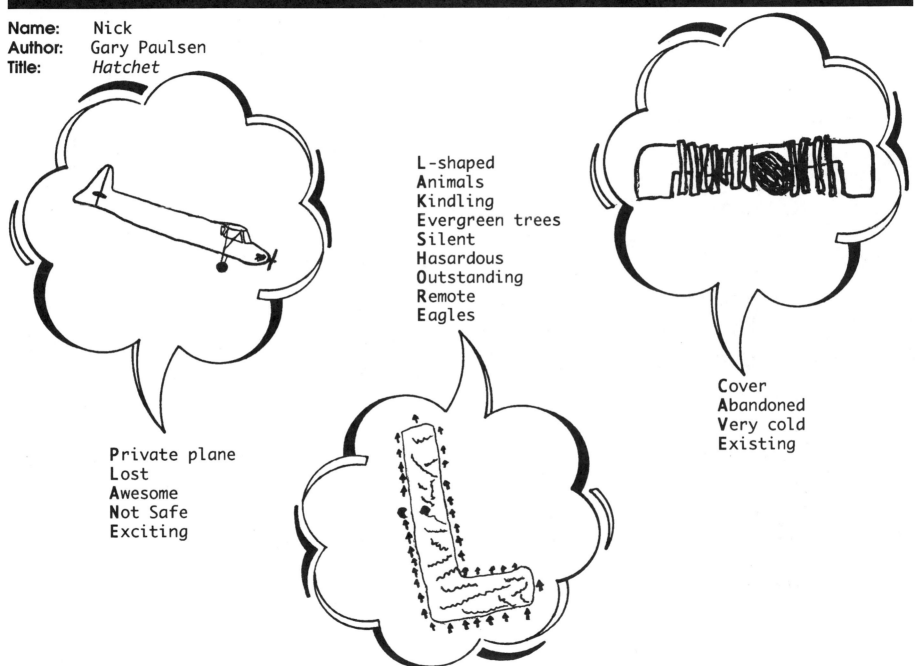

L-shaped
Animals
Kindling
Evergreen trees
Silent
Hasardous
Outstanding
Remote
Eagles

Private plane
Lost
Awesome
Not Safe
Exciting

Cover
Abandoned
Very cold
Existing

Setting Points

Lori Blevins Gonwick's fourth-grade class used her setting points idea to identify the setting specifics in <u>My Father's Dragon</u> *(see example, page 49). This technique works well with chapter books.*

Materials:
Form (copy – page 142)   Pencil/pen/markers

Goals:
To identify five settings in the story
To describe the details of each setting

Steps:
1. As you think through the story, list five of the settings in the setting points.
2. Describe the big picture on the first line of each setting point.
3. Give more setting details on the next three lines.

Writing Connection:
Imagine five different settings you would like to include in your next story

Setting Points Examples

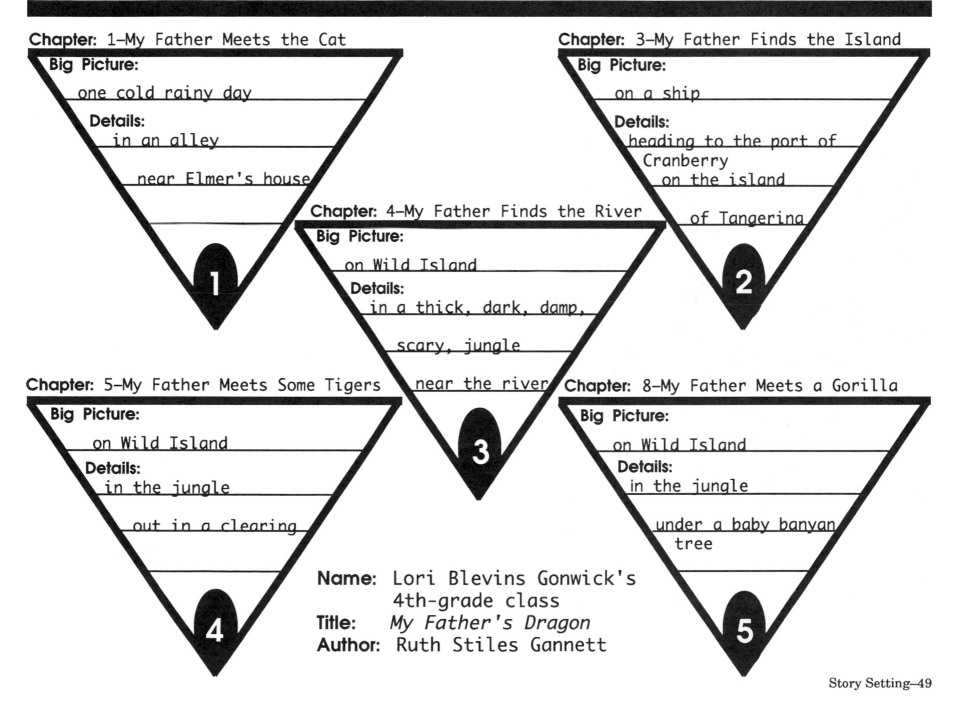

Chapter: 1—My Father Meets the Cat

Big Picture:

one cold rainy day

Details:

in an alley

near Elmer's house

1

Chapter: 3—My Father Finds the Island

Big Picture:

on a ship

Details:

heading to the port of Cranberry

on the island

of Tangerina

2

Chapter: 4—My Father Finds the River

Big Picture:

on Wild Island

Details:

in a thick, dark, damp,

scary, jungle

near the river

3

Chapter: 5—My Father Meets Some Tigers

Big Picture:

on Wild Island

Details:

in the jungle

out in a clearing

4

Chapter: 8—My Father Meets a Gorilla

Big Picture:

on Wild Island

Details:

in the jungle

under a baby banyan tree

5

Name: Lori Blevins Gonwick's 4th-grade class
Title: *My Father's Dragon*
Author: Ruth Stiles Gannett

Key Event Story Cards

Story cards are great to share with friends. Cards can be sequenced and used to retell a story. They are also fun to trade like sports cards.

Materials:

Cardstock/index cards   Pencil/pen/markers
Scissors

Goals:

To identify the key events in a story
To identify and briefly describe story settings

Steps:

1. List three to five key (important) events in the story on a separate piece of paper.
2. Cut out the number of cards you want to make out of cardstock or use index cards.
3. Draw the setting for each key event on the front of a card.
4. Write the setting information on the back.
5. Ask a friend who has read the story to identify each card's event.

Writing Connection:

Create cards for a story you are writing

Story Card Examples

Story Card
Steven
Long Shot for Pau

Key Event #9
Author: Matt Christopher
Where: At a basketball court
When: In the winter
What happened: Paul made two free shots so they won the game.

Story Card
Steven
Long Shot for Pau

Key Event #10
Author: Matt Christopher
Where: At a basketball court
When: In the winter
What happened: Paul saved the game so Don shaked his hand.

Descriptive Words Sheet

As young authors note the words and phrases others use to describe setting, they can incorporate them into their own writing. This activity fits well with the Literature Handbook in the Style Chapter, page 26 .

The Language of Authors

Describing the setting

Materials:

Paper   Pencil/pen

Goal:

To record words and phrases that painted a picture of the setting in your mind

Steps:

1. Read in the book you've selected.
2. As you re-read your book look for descriptive words and phrases describing the setting.
3. What kind of pictures do the words paint?
4. List the words and phrases you especially like on the sheet.
5. Use separate sheets for different authors, noting how they use words in unique ways.

Writing Connection:

Use your favorite words and phrases on the list to describe your own story setting

Descriptive Words Example

Words & Phrases
that create a picture of the setting

Author: Jean Craighead George
Title: Shark Beneath the Reef

stars as bright as fire

white coral beach

blue darkness

clear waters

indigo reef

deep waters

blue dolphins glowed like the sun

graceful volcano

night black • dawn gold

hot red-violet mountains

My Writing
Creating the setting

As I walked on the white coral beach, the stars as bright as fire glowed brilliantly like the sun. The deep waters of the indigo reef showed blue darkness where the blue dolphins swam.

When the sun rose the dawn gold sky and clear waters reflected the graceful volcano and the hot red-violet mountains.
Juleah Swanson

Setting Check Sheet

The mood list helps readers to start identifying the mood set by an author. It also gives readers an opportunity to evaluate the author's depiction of the setting.

Materials:
Form (copy – page 143)   Pencil/pen/markers

Goals:
To identify the setting mood
To evaluate the setting

Steps:
1. Select the story you want to evaluate.
2. Check the mood(s) that were part of the story you read.
3. Answer questions 1-3.
4. List the place, time period and mood of the story on the check sheet.
5. Draw a picture of the main setting in the box.

Writing Connections:
Select a mood for your own story from the list
Using the Check Sheet, work with a partner
 to evaluate each other's story setting

Setting Check Sheet Example

Setting Check Sheet and Mood List

Name: Annie
Title: *George and His Marvelous Medicine*
Author: Roald Dahl

Possible Setting Moods

Tense	○
Mysterious	○
Humorous	○
Frightening	○
Gloomy	○
Thrilling	○
Serene	○
Intense	○
Hopeful	○
Exciting	☑
Funny	○
Sad	○
Suspenseful	☑
Happy	☑
Unhappy	○
Scary	○
Silly	○
Lonely	○

1. How does the setting make you feel? Does it seem real to you? Yes ☑ No ☐
(Please explain on back)

2. Is it a place you would want to go? Yes ☑ No ☐
(Please explain on back)

3. The setting: __✓__ stays the same
_____ changes

Main Setting

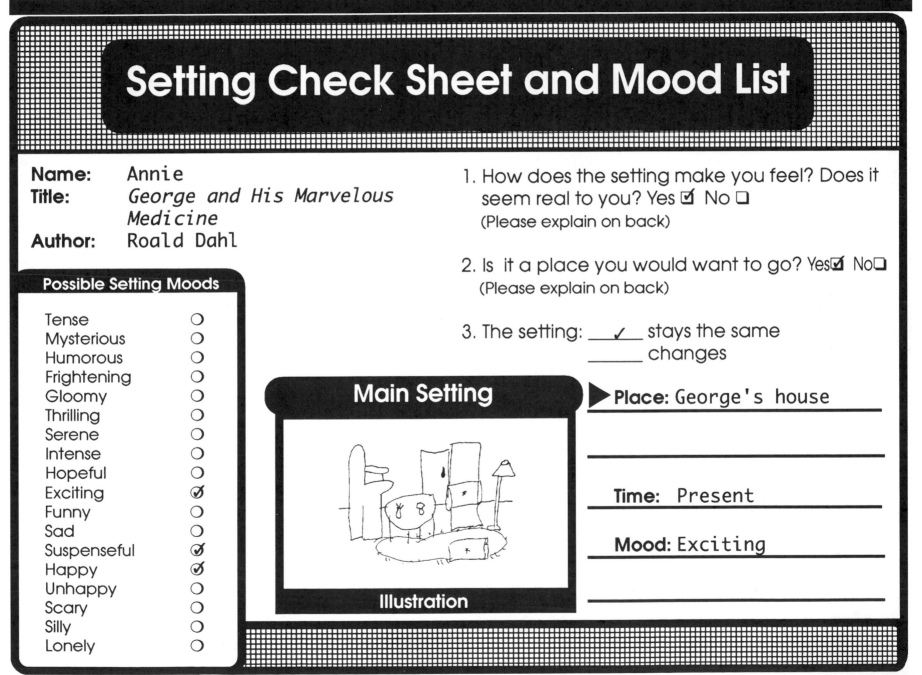

Illustration

▶ **Place:** George's house

Time: Present

Mood: Exciting

Setting Timeline and Time Capsule

The fourth graders in Valerie Marshall's and Martha Ivy's combined classroom have been reading historical fiction. The timeline example is from their students. For fun, create a string timeline to hang across a room. Attach the time capsules with tape or paper clips at the appropriate time periods.

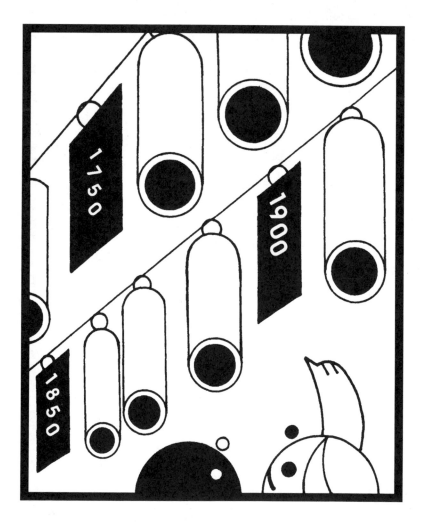

Materials:
Forms (copy – page 144)   Pencil/pen

Goals:
To record story time periods on a timeline
To briefly describe a setting in a time capsule

Steps:
1. Decide what years you want to include on your timeline.
2. Break the years down and number them in tens (see example).
3. As you finish reading a book, locate the time period on the timeline and write in the title.
4. Fill out a time capsule for each book.

Writing Connection:
Use the timeline to help you create stories which take place during different time periods

Timeline and Time Capsule Examples

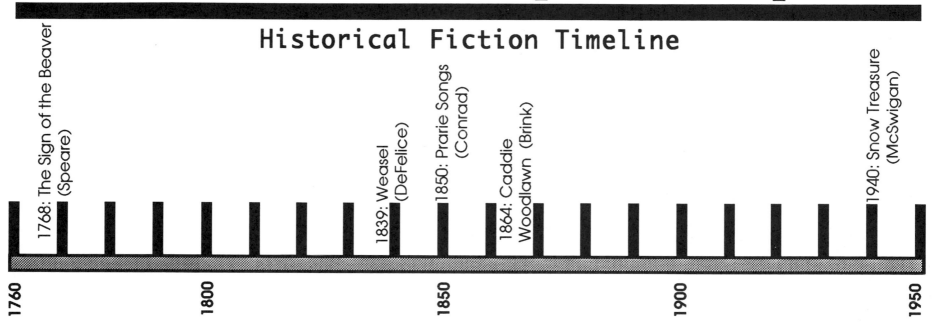

Historical Fiction Timeline

1768: The Sign of the Beaver (Speare)

1839: Weasel (DeFelice)

1850: Prarie Songs (Conrad)

1864: Caddie Woodlawn (Brink)

1940: Snow Treasure (McSwigan)

1760   1800   1850   1900   1950

Story Time Capsule for: <u>Weasel</u>

The story takes place: <u>In Minnesota</u>

The time period: <u>1839</u>

What it's like: <u>It was a rugged and hard working life. There was no electricity. You had to grow up fast. You were left alone and had</u> to be responsible for your chores.

Setting Comparison Sheet

The comparison sheet allows readers to analyze the similarities and differences between their life setting and the story setting. The 6th-grade students in Julie Neupert's class used their Comparison Setting Sheet (page 59) as a group discussion starter.

Materials:
Form (copy – page 145)   Pencil/pen

Goal:
To compare your setting to a setting in the story

Steps:
1. Choose a setting from the story.
2. List how your life and the setting are the same in the center shape.
3. Write the differences in the boxes below.
4. Discuss setting comparisons with your friends.

Writing Connection:
Change the story using your own setting instead of the setting created by the author

Setting Comparison Example

Name: 6th-graders from Ben Rush Elementary in Redmond, WA
Title: *The Cay* by Theodore Taylor

Where I live

Redmond

Story Setting

Curacao

SAME

- close to water
- some flat areas
- both have ports or harbors
- both have floating bridges

- both have things to export that the world wants
- both have business areas
- both have African Americans

DIFFERENT

Where I live		Story Setting
•cool, cloudy, rainy, moderate	**Climate**	•hot, humid
•hills, mountains, some flat	**Land**	•low, flat, small island
•moderate—larger than Curacau	**Population**	•small
•present – 1994	**Time**	•World War II, 1942
•evergreen trees	**Vegetation**	•tropical, palm trees

Select–a–Setting

It's fun to take a character into the time machine and transform the setting. It gives young authors a chance to analyze the story and write their own version.

Materials:
Form (copy – page 146)   Pencil/pen/markers

Goal:
To show how the story changes if the setting changes

Steps:
1. Choose the character you want to transport.
2. Think of a new time and place.
3. Think through how this new setting might affect the story.
4. Describe the changes this would make.
5. Predict the character's reaction to the new setting.

Writing Connection:
Re-write the story using the new setting

Select-a-Setting Example

Name: Brian
Book Title: *Babe Ruth*

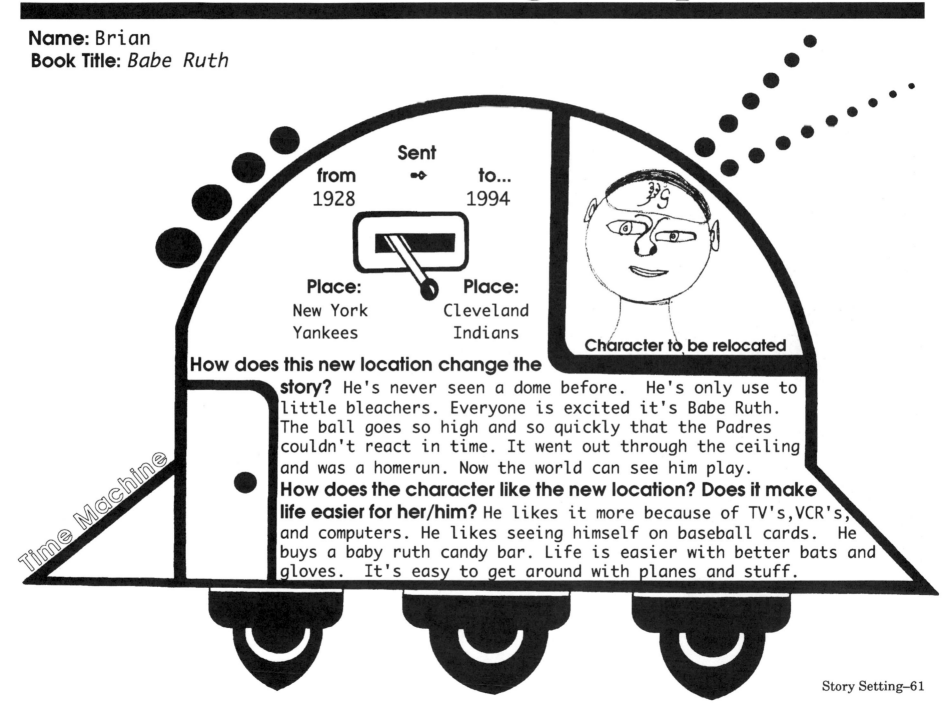

Sent

from   to...
1928   ⬥   1994

Place: Place:
New York   Cleveland
Yankees   Indians

Character to be relocated

Time Machine

How does this new location change the story? He's never seen a dome before. He's only use to little bleachers. Everyone is excited it's Babe Ruth. The ball goes so high and so quickly that the Padres couldn't react in time. It went out through the ceiling and was a homerun. Now the world can see him play.

How does the character like the new location? Does it make life easier for her/him? He likes it more because of TV's, VCR's, and computers. He likes seeing himself on baseball cards. He buys a baby ruth candy bar. Life is easier with better bats and gloves. It's easy to get around with planes and stuff.

Setting Travel Brochure

Kids find the Setting Travel Brochure irresistible. They can't wait to share their brochures with friends. Travel agents are usually eager to share brochure examples with students.

Materials:

8 1/2" x 11" paper   Pencil/pens/markers

Goal:

To create a travel brochure which will make people want to visit the setting(s)

Steps:

1. Fold your paper into three columns.
2. Draw the travel agent in column #1.
3. Draw a picture of the setting in column #2, #3, and #4. Describe the setting underneath your illustration.
4. Tell why the reader should visit this location in column #5.
5. Write your name, the date, book title and author in column #6.

Writing Connection:

Create a brochure for the setting in one of your own stories

Setting Travel Brochure Example

Outside Page

Why you should visit this setting!

Just grab the gold token from Sir Simon and shrink into a little person. It will be fun to live in a castle with a secret door, a nanny and a knight. Fight battles against the wizard Alaster with your new friends!

5.

Author: Elizabeth Winthrop

Book Title: The castle in the attic

Date: Jan 14, 1994

6.

My Name: Terry Yao

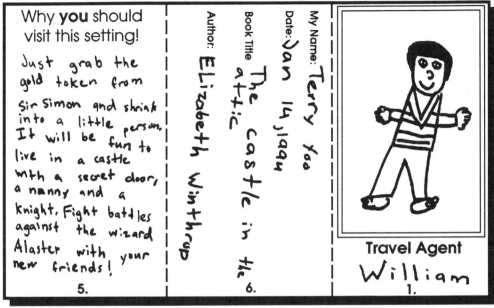

Travel Agent

William

1.

Inside Page

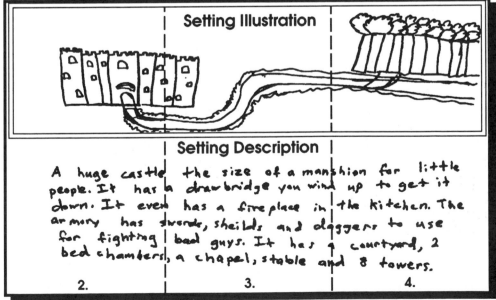

Setting Illustration

Setting Description

A huge castle the size of a manshion for little people. It has a drawbridge you wind up to get it down. It even has a fireplace in the kitchen. The armory has swords, shields and daggers to use for fighting bad guys. It has a courtyard, 2 bed chambers, a chapel, stable and 8 towers.

2.   3.   4.

Setting Journal

A setting journal is a great way to think through the setting decisions made by the author.

Materials:
Paper or Journal   Pencil/pen/markers

Goal:
To record your thoughts about the setting as you read a story

Steps:
1. Read in the book you've chosen.
2. Think about what is happening in the story right now.
3. Think about where and when the story is taking place and how the author sets the mood.
4. Write your feelings about the setting in your journal.
5. Read on in your book to see if and how the setting changes in the story.

Writing Connection:
Re-write the story changing the mood

Setting Journal Example

Possible Journal Topics

- Describe where the story is taking place.
- Tell when the story takes place and the mood of the story.
- Have you ever been to this place? If yes, when and what was it like? How was it similar to or different from the story?
- Would you like to live in this time and place? Why? How would your life be changed?
- Is the setting realistic? Why?
- What changes would you make to the setting location?
- What mood changes would you make and why?
- How would the story change if it took place in a different time?

Rene'e-Chantal
January 18, 1994
Book: *Owl Moon* by Jane Yolen

This story takes place in a snowy valley late at night, past the little girl's bedtime. I haven't been to this place but it reminds me of when I went to Colorado to see my friends.

I would like to live in this place because it is so quiet and pretty. I wish I could see a owl too.

I like this story.

Chapter 4
Story Characters

Story Characters

"I like funny characters that get into mischief and somehow get out of it on their own." Patrick Atherton, 5th grade

Characters are a very important ingredient in any story. They can help to make a story believable by drawing you into their world. Authors tell us about the characters they've created in many different ways. Some authors describe the character in detail while others leave that to your imagination. You will find stories in which characters grow and change (round characters) and others where they stay the same (flat characters). There are many ways to create characters. Successful stories are written in such a way that the characters come to life as you read the story.

In this chapter, you will have an opportunity to explore the characters in the stories you are reading. Take time to think about your favorite characters. How does the author make them so appealing? As a young author, you can use what you learn from other authors to create your own characters.

"The characters who go on adventures that bring me into the story are the greatest!"

Nick Palmer,
4th grade

"I like characters that try to solve mysteries and are always poking their nose into other people's business."

Jessica Bleeker,
6th grade

""I like baby characters and parent characters."

Michelle Short,
Kindergarten

About This Chapter

This chapter includes...

Story Characters: Explore many dimensions of story characters through...

The writing connections in each activity will help you use what you are learning about characters in your own writing.

Character Scrapbook

The Character Scrapbook is fun for all ages. It can reflect settings and events which were especially meaningful to the reader as well as important characters.

Materials:
Form (copy – page 147)   Pencil/pen/markers

Goals:
To identify story characters
To draw your image of the characters

Steps:
1. After reading a book you especially liked, draw pictures of the story characters in the squares.
2. Write the character's name underneath your drawing or have your friends guess who the character might be.
3. Share your illustrations with your friends as you tell them about each character.

Writing Connection:
Draw pictures of characters you might like to include in your own story

Character Scrapbook Example

Name: Erica
Title: *Beauty and the Beast*

Sensational Sociogram

The sociogram helps readers map out the relationships between the main character and the supporting characters. Children like to buddy up and discuss the types of relationships characters can have (enemies, teammates, etc.) and then develop characters around these relationships.

Materials:
Form (copy – page 148)   Pencil/pen/markers

Goal:
To diagram the main character's relationships to other characters in the story

Steps:
1. Write your name and the book title.
2. Draw the main character in the star.
3. Draw pictures of the other characters in the frames.
4. Write the main character's relationship to each character on the lines between the star and the frames (e.g. sister, teacher).

Writing Connection:
Use the sociogram form to show the relationships of the characters in your own story

Sensational Sociogram Example

Name: Renee-Chantal   Charlotte's Web

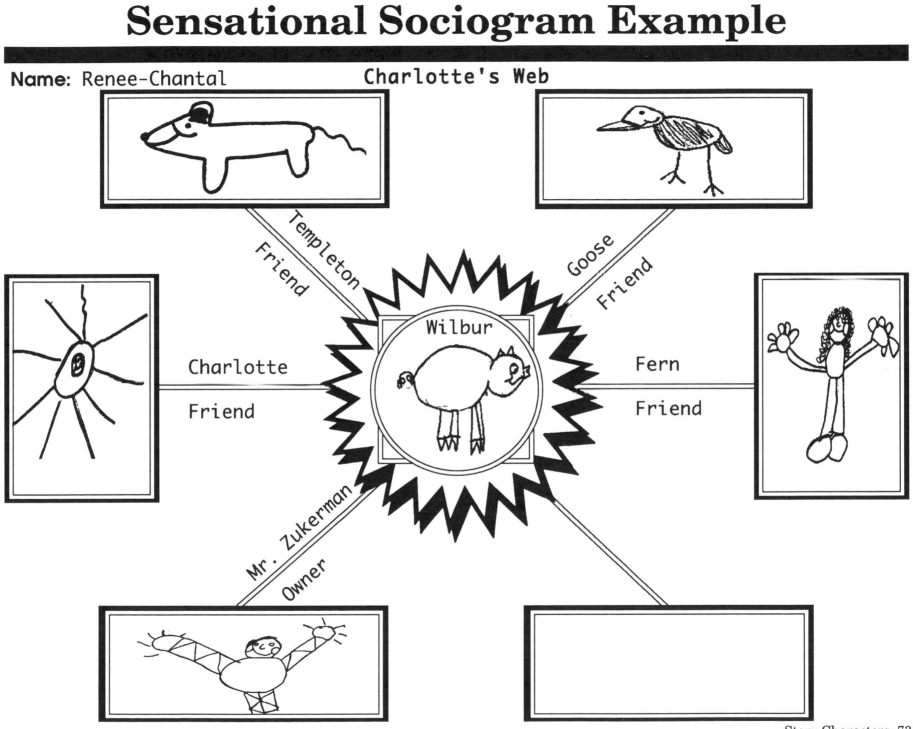

Descriptive Words Sheet

As young authors note the words and phrases others use to describe characters, they can incorporate them into their own writing. The Descriptive Words Sheet can also be used as a classroom word list with students adding to it on a daily basis after silent reading.

Materials:

Pencil/pen   Paper

Goal:

To identify words and phrases that help you to know more about the characters

Steps:

1. Read a chapter in the book you've chosen.
2. Re-read the chapter looking for descriptive words and phrases you find interesting.
3. Think about what the words tell you about the character.
4. Write the words and phrases on paper.
5. Use your sheet for different authors, noting how they use words in unique ways.

Writing Connection:

Keep a word sheet in a reading folder to record favorite phrases from your own stories

Descriptive Words Example

Philip

Descriptive Words and Phrases
that helped me get to know the
Characters

from "Touchdown for Tommy" by Matt Christopher

black sleeved grey jacket

buckled his leather hat

wants to make the catch of the day

the clothes ripped like a string of flags

orphan boy

Character Check Sheet

The character traits list helps readers to start identifying a number of common character traits. The Check Sheet gives readers an opportunity to evaluate the author's depiction of a character. Students enjoy comparing stories with flat characters to stories with round characters.

Materials:
Form (copy – page 149)   Pencil/pen/markers

Goals:
To identify the traits of a character
To evaluate how realistic the character seems

Steps:
1. Select the character you want to check.
2. Think through and answer the questions.
3. Draw a picture of the character and write in his/her traits.

Writing Connections:
Use the character traits list to help you as you create your own characters
Use the Check Sheet to evaluate your own story characters

Character Check Sheet Example

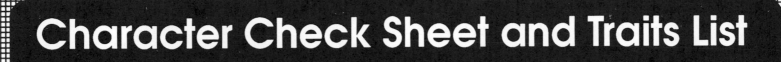

Character Check Sheet and Traits List

Name: Terry

Title: Wayside school is falling down

Common Character Traits

adventurous	friendly	pretty
awesome	fun-loving	quiet
artistic	gentle	rich
athletic	generous	respectful
active	happy	rad
beautiful	humble	sad
brave	hostile	sloppy
bold	honest	serious
bossy	intelligent	successful
cheerful	independent	shy
curious	Inventive	short
creative	leader	smart
courageous	lazy	studious
considerate	messy	selfish
daring	mischievious	simple
dreamer	mean	tall
dainty	neat	trustworthy
dangerous	nasty	thoughtful
exciting	nice	unselfish
entertaining	nosy	warm
energetic	open	witty
funny	poor	wild
fighter	proud	wonderful

1. Does the character seem real to you? Yes ☑ No ☐
(Please explain on back)

2. Do the character's actions fit what you know of him/her? Yes ☑ No ☐ (Please explain on back)

3. This character is: ___✔___ flat (stays the same)

○ round (changes)

Terrence

Character Traits

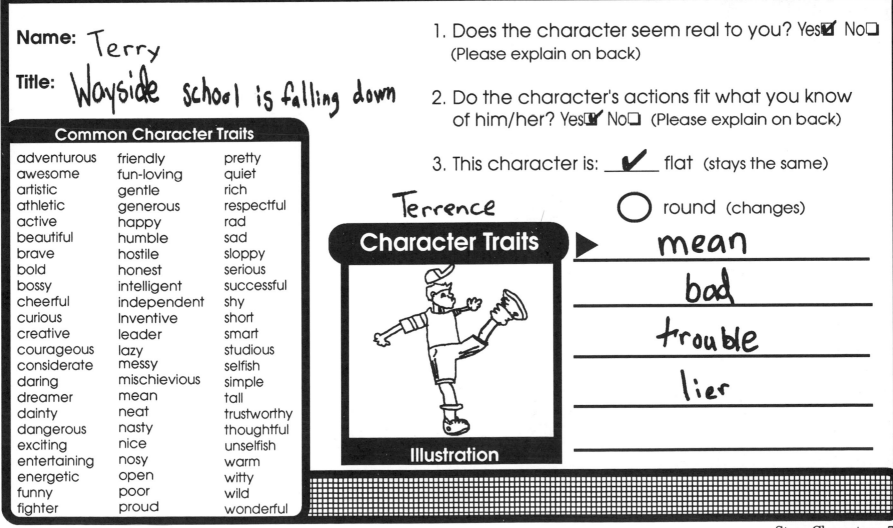

Illustration

► mean

bad

trouble

lier

Character Profile Sheet

The Character Profile can double as a Create-a-Character sheet. It is a great way for young authors to develop characters they will use in their own stories. This sheet can also be used in creating a biographical profile of a real person.

Materials:

Form (copy – page 150)　　Pencil/pen/markers

Goals:

To imagine a story character is a real person
To answer questions as if you were the
　character

Steps:

1. Select a character for your profile.
2. Remember what the author has written about the character.
3. Imagine that you are the character as you answer the profile questions.
4. Compare profiles of the same character with a friend.

Writing Connection:

Use the profile as a guide to help you create
　your own characters

Character Profile Example

Annie

Character Name:
Matilda

Personal Information

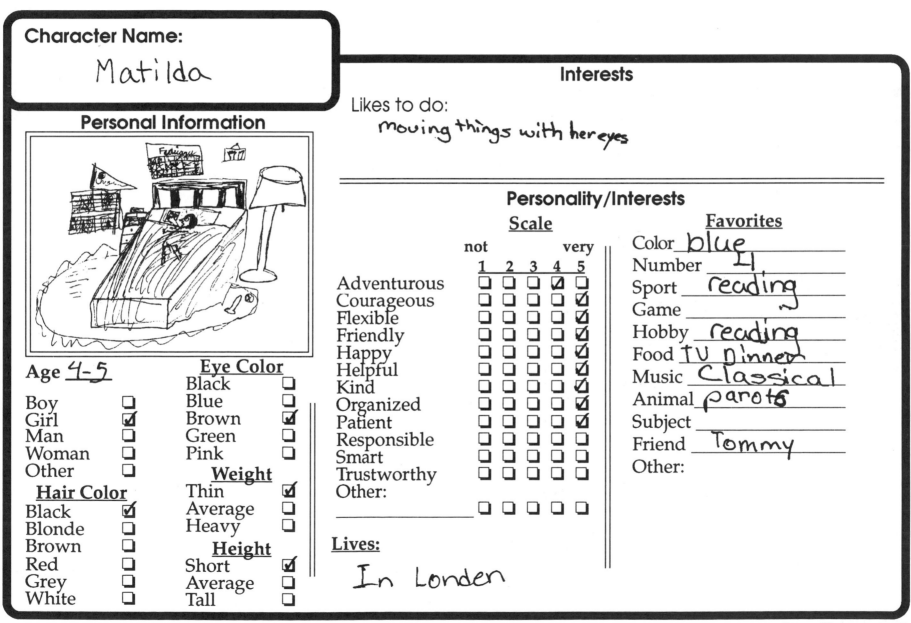

Age 4-5

		Eye Color	
		Black	☐
Boy	☐	Blue	☐
Girl	☑	Brown	☑
Man	☐	Green	☐
Woman	☐	Pink	☐
Other	☐		

Hair Color

		Weight	
Black	☑	Thin	☑
Blonde	☐	Average	☐
Brown	☐	Heavy	☐
Red	☐	**Height**	
Grey	☐	Short	☑
White	☐	Average	☐
		Tall	☐

Interests

Likes to do:
moving things with her eyes

Personality/Interests

Scale

	not				very
	1	2	3	4	5
Adventurous	☐	☐	☐	☑	☐
Courageous	☐	☐	☐	☐	☑
Flexible	☐	☐	☐	☐	☑
Friendly	☐	☐	☐	☐	☑
Happy	☐	☐	☐	☐	☑
Helpful	☐	☐	☐	☐	☑
Kind	☐	☐	☐	☐	☑
Organized	☐	☐	☐	☐	☑
Patient	☐	☐	☐	☐	☑
Responsible	☐	☐	☐	☐	☐
Smart	☐	☐	☐	☐	☐
Trustworthy	☐	☐	☐	☐	☐
Other: _____	☐	☐	☐	☐	☐

Favorites
Color blue
Number 4
Sport reading
Game
Hobby reading
Food TV Dinner
Music Classical
Animal parots
Subject
Friend Tommy
Other:

Lives:

In London

Character Map

The Character Map is a fun way to explore many different aspects of a character. As students identify the feelings, behavior, and personality traits of characters developed by other authors, they can start to incorporate more complex characters into their own stories.

Materials:
Form (copy – page 151)   Pencil/pen/markers

Goal:
To identify different parts of a character

Steps:
1. Select a character for your map.
2. Write the character's name in the center circle and/or draw a picture of him/her.
3. Describe the character in box 2.
4. Think about the feelings the character experienced, his/her behavior, personality and actions.
5. List feelings in box 1, behavior in box 3, and personality traits in box 4.

Writing Connection:
Create and explore your own story character using the character map

Character Map Example

Name: Juleah

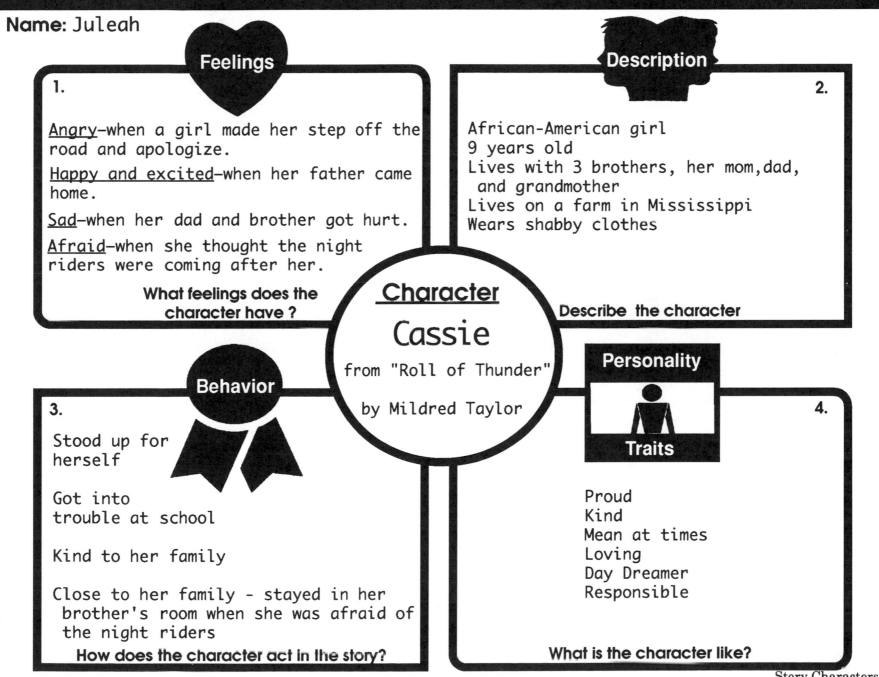

Feelings

1.

Angry—when a girl made her step off the road and apologize.

Happy and excited—when her father came home.

Sad—when her dad and brother got hurt.

Afraid—when she thought the night riders were coming after her.

What feelings does the character have ?

Description

2.

African-American girl
9 years old
Lives with 3 brothers, her mom, dad, and grandmother
Lives on a farm in Mississippi
Wears shabby clothes

Describe the character

Character

Cassie

from "Roll of Thunder"

by Mildred Taylor

Behavior

3.

Stood up for herself

Got into trouble at school

Kind to her family

Close to her family - stayed in her brother's room when she was afraid of the night riders

How does the character act in the story?

Personality

Traits

4.

Proud
Kind
Mean at times
Loving
Day Dreamer
Responsible

What is the character like?

Char-a-Graph

Julie Neupert's sixth-grade students helped to design and name the Char-a-Graph. Other students have really enjoyed graphing how characters change within a story using this graph.

Materials:
Form (copy – page 152)   Pencil

Goal:
To show how characters change in a story

Steps:
1. Choose the character and trait you want to show on your char-a-graph.
2. List 5 key ♀ events in the story on a separate sheet of paper.
3. List five levels of the trait you selected to the left of the thermometer (see example).
4. Select a trait level for each key event. Draw a dot above each event at its trait level.
5. Connect the dots to show how the character did or didn't change through the story.

Writing Connection:
With a friend, make a list of different feelings to use with characters in your own story

Char-a-Graph Example

Name: Steven   **Title:** The kid who only hit homers

Character: Sylvester

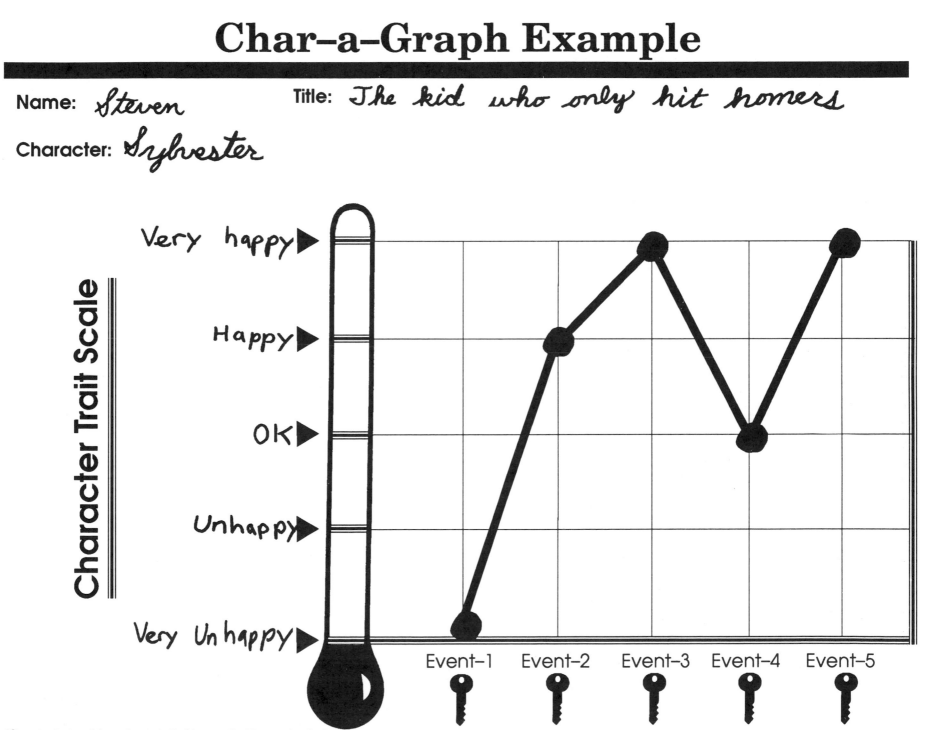

(Graph design ideas from Julie Neupert's 6th-grade students)

Character Journal

A character journal provides an opportunity for students to express their personal connection to the characters in a story. It can also be used as a springboard for character development in their own stories.

Caddie Woodlawn

Materials:

Paper or Journal   Pencil/pen

Goal:

To compare yourself to a character in the story

Steps:

1. Read in the book you've chosen.
2. Think about what the author has told you about the character so far.
3. Think about what you have in common with the character.
4. Think about how you are different.
5. Compare yourself to the character in your journal.

Writing Connection:

Create a story in which the main character is very similar to you

Character Journal Example

Possible Journal Topics

- What things do you have in common with the character?
- How are you different?
- What do you like about the character? (Explain)
- What don't you like? Why?
- Would you like to be friends with this character?(Explain)
- Do you approve of the character's behavior? Why?
- Does the character remind you of someone you know?
- Does the character seem real to you? How did the author help to make this character seem real?
- Compare your life to his/hers.
- How would you change the character?

Nick
February 28, 1994
Book: *The Return of the Indian*

My favorite character in the story is Little Bear. He is three inches tall. We are both boys. He is about 30 years old and I am almost ten.

He is my favorite because he's the main character and I think he's cool.

I like it when he's nice to Omri and Patrick. I don't like it when he is rude sometimes like when he yells.

I think the author did a good job in making him because he seems real to me.

If I could change Little Bear I would make him as tall as a real human.

Chapter 5
Story Plot

Story Plot

"I like surprises in stories. I liked <u>Karen's Big Joke</u>, because her family played a big joke on her." Emily Gibbons, 2nd grade

Plot is how the story unfolds. It includes the problems and solutions created by authors to make the story exciting. Many times story characters face conflict and problems just like we do in our lives. This helps us to relate to the character. A successful story makes you feel as if you are personally experiencing the story; you are in the story.

Plots usually follow a pattern and rely upon four basic types of conflict: character against character, character against the environment, character against society and character against self.

In this chapter you will discover many fun and different ways to look at a story's plot. Try writing your own front-page news story or creating a filmstrip story sequencer. Use what you learn from your favorite authors to write stories that will keep your reader on the edge of his seat!

""Sequencing a story is like putting a puzzle together."

Travis Calhoun, 4th grade

"Without a plot a story would stay on the same level of excitement, with no beginning, middle, and end."

Garett Reece, 5th grade

"I like books that have exciting problems and mostly happy endings."

Tara O'Brien, 3rd grade

About This Chapter

This chapter includes...

Plot Development: Explore many dimensions of story plot through...

The writing connections in each activity will help you use what you are learning about story plot in your own writing.

Filmstrip Story Sequencer

Lori Blevins Gonwick's filmstrip story sequencer idea is a big hit with her fourth-grade students. It is a great individual, buddy, or group activity. Lori created a huge filmstrip with 8 1/2" x 11" openings. It hangs on the wall in her classroom.

Materials:
Form (copy – page 153)   Pencil/pens/markers

Goals:
To identify and sequence the events in a story
To retell a story you really liked

Steps:
1. Write the book title, author, your name and the date in strip #1.
2. Decide upon the number of key events you want to include in your filmstrip.
3. Determine the order of your key events.
4. Draw a picture of each event in the filmstrip openings using the order you determined above.
5. Share your filmstrip sequencer with others by retelling the story.

Filmstrip Story Sequencer Example

Davy's Dream by Paul Owen Lewis

1. DAVY'S DREAM BY DANNY McCARTHY

2. Davy dreams and looks at harbor

3. He dreams of sailing with orcas

4. He paints his boat like an orca

5. Davy sails his boat into water

6. Orcas carry his boat to safety

Story Train

Younger children find the story train is a fun way to sequence the events in a story. It also helps them to identify the beginning, middle, and end of a story. It is a great tool for retelling a story.

Materials:
Form (copy – page 154)   Pencil/pen/markers

Goals:
To identify a story's beginning, middle and end
To retell the story

Steps:
1. Think about what happened in the beginning of the story and draw it in the first car of the train.
2. Draw a picture of what happened next in the second car.
3. Draw what happened last in the third car.
4. Share your drawings with your friends as you tell them about the story.

Writing Connection:
Use the story train as a pre-write in which you draw the beginning, middle and end of your own story

Story Train Example

Name: Renee-Chantal
Title: *Christmas Moon* by Denys Cazet

What happened first?   **What happened next?**   **What happened last?**

Beginning   **Middle**   **End**

Description: In the beginning, the little rabbit can't get to sleep. He can't stop thinking about his grandpa. In the middle, his mom is telling him about his grandpa and he remembers everything he did with his grandpa and what he won. In the end, his mom tucks him in and he falls asleep thinking about Christmas.

Story Comic Strip

Kids love to create comic strips. It is a fun way to start writing dialogue and helps students to sequence story events.

Materials:
Pen/pencil/markers   Paper

Goals:
To show story plot development through comic strip sequences
To retell the important events in the story

Steps:
1. Write a list of the key events in the story.
2. Put the events in order.
3. Count up the key events to determine how many frames you will include.
4. Draw each event with dialogue inside or below the comic strip box.

Writing Connections:
Use your imagination to create your own comic strip as a pre-write for your story
Create a comic strip with the same characters in a new adventure

Story Comic Strip Example

Name: Juleah

"Can you read minds?"

"I can see in the dark and move things without touching them."

"Let's move the bag to the door."

"CRASH!"

"Let's get out of here."

"It was that weird girl with the silver eyes!"

Story Map

The children in Suzie Fiebig's second-grade classroom use this story map to identify a story's characters and setting as well as its problems and solutions. They also use it as a pre-write for stories that they create. Yufanyi's pre-write example was patterned after the story, _Frog and Toad_. She went on to write her own sequel using this pre-write.

Materials:
Form (copy – page 155)   Pencil/pen

Goal:
To record the main elements in a story

Steps:
1. Select the book you want to use in your map.
2. Think about each box.
3. Fill in the information.
4. Re-tell the story to a friend using the information from your map.

Writing Connection:
Use the map as a pre-write for the next story you write (see example)

Story Map Example

Main Characters

frog
toad

Setting

toad in bed

Supporting Characters

Title and Author
toad in bed
by
Yufanyi

Problem

frog woned to play

toad was slepey

he wanded to slep

toad playd joks

Solution

then frog and toad playd

Toad in Bed
by Yufanyi

Once upon a time there lived to frogs. Their names were Frog and Toad. Frog loved to play. Toad loved to sleep. And that is how my story begins. One day Frog siad can you play today? Toad siad I'm sleepy, mayby tomorrow siad Frog but but Toad did not answer. Frog was scared. Toad came up and turned on the light and Toad said... boooo! Frog was scared. He siad don't do that! Toad siad sorry. Frog siad it's ok and Frog siad would you like to play? Toad siad yes! Then Toad and Frog would play. The next morning Frog was sad. Toad asked "what's the matter. Frog didn't answer. Frog siad "were are you? Toad didn't answer. Toad was playing another jok on Frog. Frog siad Toad never learns. The End.

Problem & Solution Diagram

Carol Fletcher's third-grade students used the Problem & Solution Diagram to discuss <u>Charlotte's Web</u> (see example).

Materials:

Form (copy – page 156)   Pencil/pen

Goals:

To identify the main problem and solution
To identify the main character's goal
To identify key events in the story

Steps:

1. Think about the story.
2. What is the big problem?
3. What is the main goal?
4. What were three important things that happened related to the problems?
5. How was the problem resolved?
6. Write your answers in the map.

Writing Connection:

Use this story map as a pre-write to help you think through your next story

Problem & Solution Diagram Example

Book Title: *Charlotte's Web*

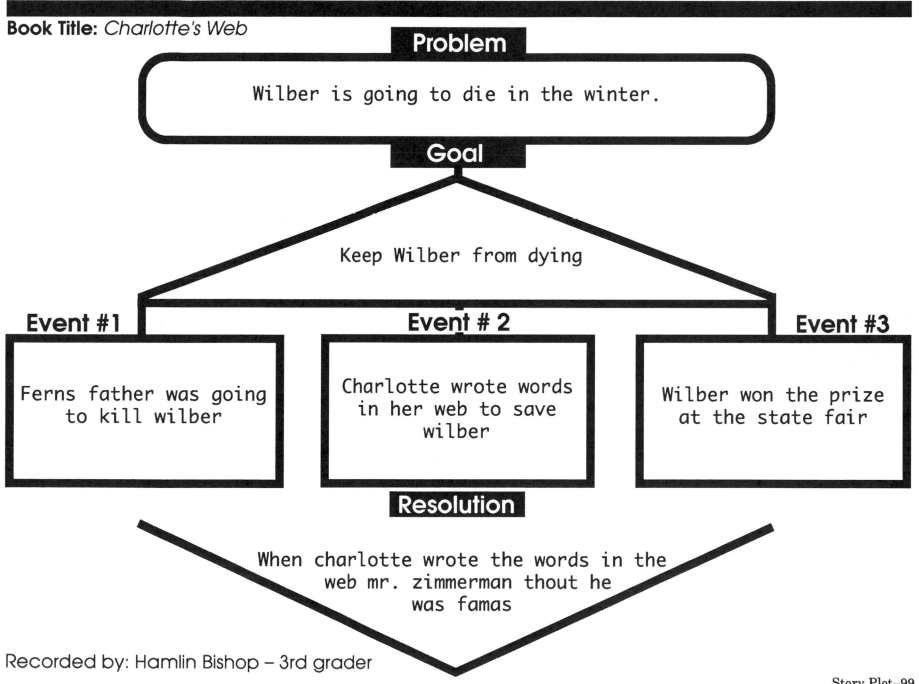

Problem

Wilber is going to die in the winter.

Goal

Keep Wilber from dying

Event #1

Ferns father was going to kill wilber

Event # 2

Charlotte wrote words in her web to save wilber

Event #3

Wilber won the prize at the state fair

Resolution

When charlotte wrote the words in the web mr. zimmerman thout he was famas

Recorded by: Hamlin Bishop – 3rd grader

Plot Check Sheet

The conflict list helps readers to start identifying the types of conflict found in stories. It also gives readers an opportunity to evaluate the author's plot development.

Materials:
Form (copy – page 157)   Pencil/pen

Goals:
To identify the story's type(s) of conflict
To evaluate the plot of the story

Steps:
1. Think about the plot of the story you've selected.
2. Determine the type(s) of conflict in the story and check the boxes which fit.
3. Answer questions 1–3 on the form.
4. List the main problem, main character's goal and how the problem was resolved.

Writing Connections:
Use the conflict list to help identify the type of conflict you want to include in your story
Evaluate the plot of your own story with a partner

Plot Check Sheet Example

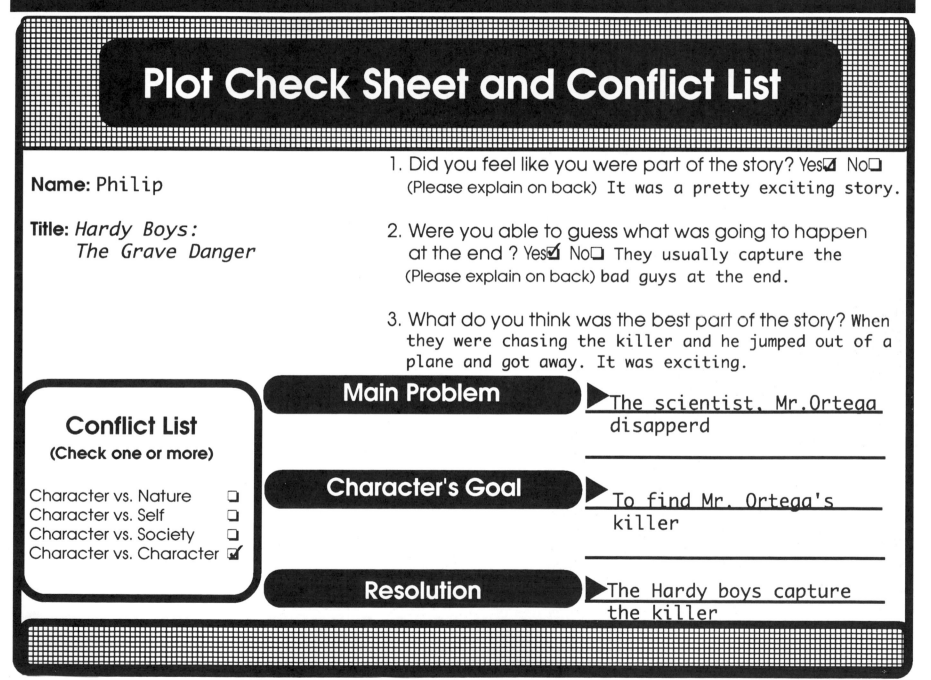

Plot Check Sheet and Conflict List

Name: Philip

Title: *Hardy Boys:*
The Grave Danger

1. Did you feel like you were part of the story? Yes☑ No☐
(Please explain on back) It was a pretty exciting story.

2. Were you able to guess what was going to happen
at the end ? Yes☑ No☐ They usually capture the
(Please explain on back) bad guys at the end.

3. What do you think was the best part of the story? When
they were chasing the killer and he jumped out of a
plane and got away. It was exciting.

Conflict List
(Check one or more)

Character vs. Nature ☐
Character vs. Self ☐
Character vs. Society ☐
Character vs. Character ☑

Main Problem ▶ The scientist, Mr.Ortega disapperd

Character's Goal ▶ To find Mr. Ortega's killer

Resolution ▶ The Hardy boys capture the killer

Graph-a-Plot

Graphing conflict, climax and resolution is a very visual method of identifying plot development. It is a fun individual, partner and group activity. Students find it interesting to compare the graphs from different stories. See glossary for definitions (page 20-21).

Materials:
Form (copy – page 158)   Pencil

Goal:
To graph a story's conflict and its resolution

Steps:
1. Choose the story you want to graph.
2. List 5 key events in the story on a separate sheet of paper.
3. Place the events in order from 1 to 5.
4. Place a dot above each event at the conflict level that fits on the conflict thermometer.
5. Connect the dots to show how the conflict builds and resolves.
6. List the key events on the graph (as shown).

Writing Connection:
Apply the same pattern of building conflict and resolution into a story you are writing

Graph-a-Plot Example

Name: Terry
Title: *Castle in the Attic*

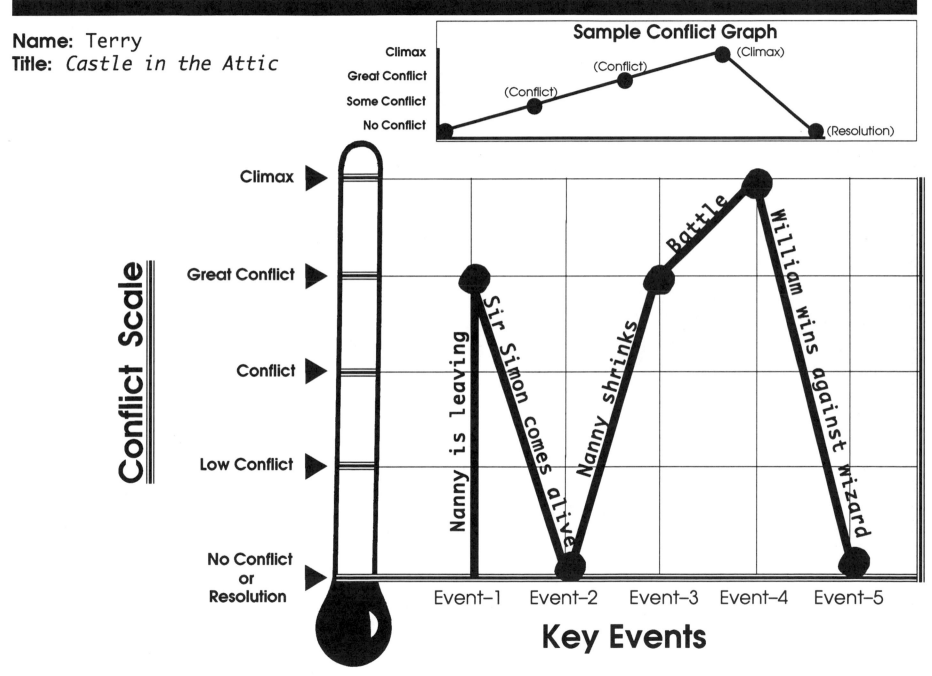

Sample Conflict Graph

Climax
Great Conflict
Some Conflict
No Conflict

(Conflict)
(Conflict)
(Climax)
(Resolution)

Conflict Scale

Climax ▶
Great Conflict ▶
Conflict ▶
Low Conflict ▶
No Conflict or Resolution ▶

Nanny is leaving
Sir Simon comes alive
Nanny shrinks
Battle
William wins against wizard

Event–1   Event–2   Event–3   Event–4   Event–5

Key Events

Book Jacket

Lori Blevins Gonwick's fourth-grade class shared their book jacket idea with new friends in a classroom from Pittsburgh, PA. Both classrooms had a great time creating book jackets. Most classrooms laminate the finished jackets to protect them.

Materials:

Large construction paper (22" by 81/2")
Pencil/pen/markers

Goals:

To design a new cover for a book
To summarize a story

Steps:

1. Choose the book for your cover design.
2. Fold your paper in half, and then fold the last 3" of each half toward the inside to create the two inside flaps and the cover.
3. Illustrate the covers. Then write the title, author, and a summary of the story on the right flap. Write about yourself on the left flap.

Writing Connection:

Design your own unique cover and use it to inspire a story you will write

Book Jacket Example

This "It Wasn't My Fault' book jacket was created by Hope Christensen

About
the
Book Jacket
Designer

My name is Hope. My family is my Mom, Dad, Nick, Jan, and Me.
I live in a house in Kirkland, Washington. My favorite food is a hot dog. I like to play ball. I love me!

It Wasn't My Fault
by
Helen Lester

It Wasn't My Fault
by
Helen Lester

Things always went wrong with Murdley's Grandson. A bird can hold an egg on his head.
He thought it was his fault but it wasn't.
A big bird laid his egg because it was dark and scarey.
The bird made a big noise because the hippo stepped on his tail.
The hippo stepped on his tail because a rabbit in a shoe scared him.

Right Side Panel   Back Cover   Front Cover   Left Side Panel

Front – Page News Story

News stories are fun and informative. Two students in Joyce Standing's fifth-grade class chose to write news stories based on the books they just finished reading (see examples on page 107).

Materials:
Paper
Pencil

Goal:
To summarize the story in a news article

Steps:
1. Choose the book for your news story.
2. Look at the front page headlines in a newspaper and read the articles.
3. Do you notice a pattern in the articles?
4. Recreate that pattern (see examples) in your own front–page news story.
5. Remember to answer a reporter's questions: Who? What? Where? When? How? and Why?

Front – Page News Story Examples

DAILY PLANET NEWS

Canada, 1990
by Michael Armstrong
Daily Planet News Reporter

Three Inch Tall Men Brought to Life with a Key in the Cupboard!

3 inch tall men from cowboy and indian times come to life with the turn of a key! An indian brave named Little Bear, and a cowboy named Boone. These little men were brought to life by Omri. A young regular boy. Omri kept them secret for about two years. Within those two years, Omri had many exciting adventures. Also as it turns out these two men actully were real people in thier own times! The second thing Omri discovered was that he could bring any plastic figure to life with his cupboard and key. At one point Little Bear shot Boone in the chest with one of his arrows while Omri and his friend were watching a country western movie on the television, wich Boone and Little Bear had never seen before. So Omri did the only thing he could do bring a doctor to life. That is how Tommy, a world war two doctor, after finishing his job, went back to his own time, and the world war.

Continued on page A 12

The Return of the Indian by Lynne Reid Banks

THE NEW YORK TIMES
Saturday

MUSIC at the Metropolitan Museum of Modern Art?

New York, New York
by C.P. Waite
New York Times Reporter

FOUND at the Metropolitan Museum of Modern Art. A violin case and trumpet case. There are names on them. Claudia is on the violin case, Jaime is on the trumpet case. We predict they had been there for about one week because there was a layer of dust on them. Please call 343- MOMA to claim.

From the Mixed-Up Files of Mrs. Basil E. Frankweiler by E.L. Konigsburg

Character Advice Journal

A character advice journal is a great way to brainstorm options and solutions to problems faced by the character in a story. It is also fun to see if characters are making the same decisions you would.

Materials:

Paper or Journal   Pencil/pen

Goal:

To give problem-solving advice to a character as you read a story

Steps:

1. Read in the book you've chosen.
2. Think about what is happening in the story right now.
3. Think about what you would do if you were in the same situation as the character.
4. Write advice to the character in your journal.
5. Read on in your book to see how the character's decisions are similar to and different from your suggestions.

Writing Connection:

Re-write the story using your journal entries to change solutions and endings.

Character Advice Journal Example

Possible Journal Topics

- What problem does the character face right now?
- Have you ever faced this problem? If yes, what did you do?
- What are the character's options?
- Which option would you take?
- How would you change his or her behavior?
- What do you think will happen next?
- Is the character following your advice?
- What should the character do now?
- Do his/her actions make sense to you?

Brian
December 15, 1993
Book: *Dragon Wings*

Moonshadow faces the white Americans nextstore. The group throws stones, food and also punchs him.

I have had problems like this before too. I did nothing till some kids threw stones and hit me in the head. Then I threw them back.

You could throw rocks back, do nothing or you could move away - back to the Company.

Maybe you should stay in the house till the mean nextstore neighbors move.

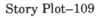

Chapter 6

Projects Recommended by Kids

Projects Recommended by Kids

"I'd like to cut out magazine objects which represent my favorite character and use them in a character collage." Carly White, 6th grade

Projects are fun. The projects listed in this chapter were all highly recommended by the kids involved in the creation of this book. They were asked to share their personal and classroom favorites with *Read & Write* readers. The projects that are included in this chapter are those they felt were the most fun to create around the characters, setting, and plots in the books they read and the books they write.

There are many different projects in this chapter. Try painting a t-shirt of a character from a book you've written or write a monologue to share with your friends. Take a look at the ABC Book example by fourth-graders based on the Oregon Trail and write your own book using another topic.

We hope you enjoy these projects and use them to help you create your own projects!

"I'd like to create a t-shirt with Babe Herman from the book, *Baseball Personalities,* on it."

Gavin Schroder, 5th grade

"I've done a diorama before and I liked creating the setting. The setting was a lot of fun!"

Matt Palmer, 4th grade

"It was fun doing the Setting Travel Brochure. My example is on page 63!"

Terry Yoo, 3rd grade

"If I made a t-shirt, It would have Mickey Mouse on it."

Erica Reiling, Kindergarten

About This Chapter

This chapter includes...

Fun with Projects: Explore story elements through...

Project List

The Project List helps readers keep track of the various projects they've already completed. It also helps them select a new project. The Project Supply Sheet on page 132 will help readers organize their projects.

Materials:
Form (copy – page 115)   Pencil/pen

Goals:
To record the projects you've completed and
  their book titles
To help you select a project idea

Steps:
1. Use the project list to select your project.
2. Look up the directions on the "RW" page #.
3. Mark an X in the project box after you complete your project.
4. Write the book title and completion date.
5. Place a star by a project you especially liked.

Writing Connection:
Use the projects with the stories you've written
  instead of another author's writing

Project List

RW Page	Project									
130	ABC Book									
104	Book Jacket									
122	Character Business Card									
70	Character Scrapbook									
118	Diorama									
106	Front–Page News Story									
50	Key Event Story Cards									
117	Mobile									
120	Monolgue									
124	Real Estate Brochure									
94	Story Comic Strip									
126	3-D Project									
128	T-Shirt Project									
56	Timeline									
56	Time Capsule									
62	Travel Brochure									

Story Mobile

The Story Mobile was recommended by Julie Neupert's sixth graders. This project can highlight characters, setting, or key events.

Materials:

White paper	Pencil/pens/markers
Yarn	Glue
Index card	Hanger

Goal:

To create and display characters from a story

Steps:

1. List the main characters on a sheet of paper.
2. Draw each character (3" tall) on white paper with his/her name placed at the feet.
3. Draw both the front and back sides.
4. Cut strips of yarn to hang the characters on the hangers.
5. Glue a piece of yarn to each character.
6. Attach each character by tying the top of the yarn to the hanger.
7. Write your name, book title, and author on an index card and attach it to the hanger.

Mobile Directions

Step 1 and Step 2

Draw each character (3") on a sheet of white paper. Cut the characters out.

Step 3

Draw on front and back sides.

Step 4

Cut pieces of yarn for each character.

Step 5

Glue yarn to the character's head.

Step 6

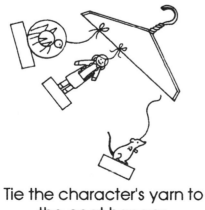

Tie the character's yarn to the coat hanger.

Step 7

Yufanyi

Charlotte's Web
by
E.B. White

Write your name, the book title and author on an index card.

Mobile Example

Display your finished mobile for others to see.

Diorama

The Diorama was recommended by students in Suzie Fiebig's second-grade class. The example is from a group of students who worked together to create a diorama. This project highlights setting and characters.

Materials:

Shoebox	Crayons/markers
Scissors	Glue
Cloth/String	Clay

Goal:

To create a model of the setting and characters from a story

Steps:

1. Select the book you want to use.
2. Turn your shoebox on its side.
3. Select a scene you really enjoyed from the book.
4. Using cloth, string, pieces of paper and other materials create the scene inside the box.
5. Using paper or clay create the characters.
6. Write your name, the book title, author, and information about the book on an index card. Tape it to the top of the box.

Diorama Directions

Step 1

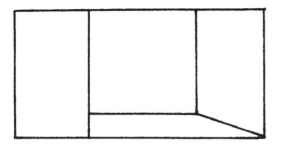

Find a shoe box for your diorama.

Step 2 and Step 3

Draw the characters you want in your diorama and cut them out.

Step 4

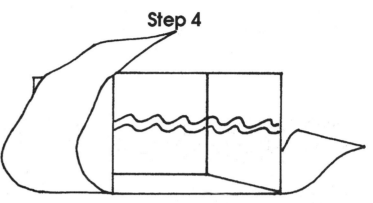

Cover the box with construction paper and draw the setting on the inside.

Step 5

Tie the characters to a piece of yarn if you want them to float or fly in the air. Glue other characters to the inside.

Step 6

Whales are mammals. They
breath air. They are not
like fish. Fish breath
water and whales are warm
bloded animals.
by Matt Hali Margaret
   Katie John

Write information about the book you read on the index card and tape it to the top of the shoe box.

Diorama Example

Share your finished diorama.

Story Monologue

Joyce Standing's fifth-grade class recommended the Story Monologue as a great project. The examples on page are monologues of two students from the class. They were a hit. A monologue is a great way to integrate reading and writing. This project highlights characters and plot.

Materials:

Paper   Pencil/pen/markers

Goal:

To create a speech that has something to do with a book and is to be read by one person

Steps:

1. Select a story.
2. Think about what you would like to share from this book. It could be a speech about the author or a section of the story played out by one of the characters (see examples)
3. Determine what your focus will be.
4. Write your speech (monologue).
5. Present your monologue to your friends.
6. You can also create props to go with your monologue as Carie did in her example.

Monologue Examples

MY PLAN TO RUN AWAY

Introduction Card

MY PLAN
TO
RUN AWAY

Card 1

Destination: M.O.M.A.
Departure time: When we
            leave for
            school
Departure day: Wednesday

Card 2

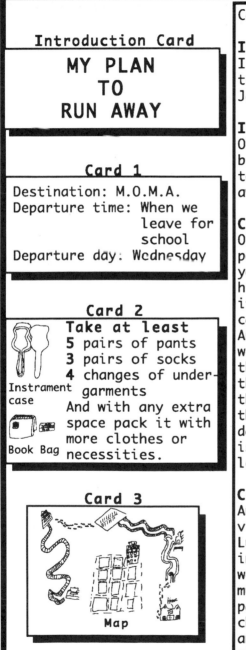

Instrament case

Book Bag

**Take at least
5** pairs of pants
3 pairs of socks
4 changes of undergarments
And with any extra space pack it with more clothes or necessities.

Card 3

Map

Carie Towler

Introduction:
I'd like to tell you that I'm pretending to talk to my little brother Jamie and the class.

Introduction Card:
Oh, Jamie now we're going to have to be quiet because we don't want mom to hear so here it is my plan to run away.

Card 1:
Okay, our destination is the Metropolitan museum of modern art. Do you know why I chose that place to hide out in? I chose it because it's a warm shelter and if we're careful we'll never get cught. Anyways, our departure time is when we leave for school. Do you know the answer to this question? I think not. We leave then because they'll never notice us walking out the door! And finally our departure day is Wednesday because Wednesday is music lesson day. And music lesson day means instrument cases!

Card 2:
And what can instrument cases provide for us? Lugege! You see our Lugege will be our book bags and our instrument cases. You see this way we won't be noticed. Oh yeah, you must take at least five pairs of pants, six pairs of socks, four changes of undergarments, six shirts and with any leftover space pack it with necesities.   Over---

---

David Waldbaum

Eulogy for Mr. Roald Dahl by a Childhod Friend

I have been chosen to do a eulogy for Mr. Roald Dahl, whom you must know; was an extraordinary man and boy. His childhood is my greatest focus for then I knew him best. His writings are of the greatest books for children everywhere. His childhood inspired him in his books that include laughter, pain, fiction and most of all, they capture your child and take him or her to wonderous places.

I close my eyes and I clearly remember five of us boys and a ingenious idea to shock the grungy, grimy, grotesque candy store owner, Mrs. Prachett. We dreaded this awful woman who was always complaining. This idea was from the master-mind, Roald himself. You see we hid our prized possessions, which were loads of candy, undernieth a floor bourd in the back of the classroom. One day, a dead mouse was spotted on my pile of Licorice Bootlaces. I was throwing it out the window when Roald suddenly yelped "Wait." Oh, did he have a vigorous but joyous enlightment in his eyes! Roald's great plot was to drop the dead mouse in the giant gobstoppers jar. He had the honor of this deed. Why do you ask would we go every day to this candy store? Because every one of us had a craving to have all this candy, not to nessesarly eat but to be proud to own it. We were taken from class and beaten with a large cane for the first time with Mrs. Prachett watching, and cheering while the Headmaster struck our behinds. In his book Matilda similar things happen with the same amount of emotion. I am proud of Roald for at Repton he was ready to become a Boazer, he turned it down for he could not beat a fog for wrongdoings or lazy workmanship. All of this is only one memory, only one story. I could talk for days and days about Mr. Roald Dahl.

Roald inspired my life for I will continue to enjoy every second of it just like him. If not now, when? I am 74 years old. My friends absense is worse than his departure. I read his books at night so I'm not alone, not fully.

Character Business Card

Lori Blevins Gonwick's fourth graders recommended her business card idea. The fourth graders in Martha Ivy's and Valerie Marshall's classroom used the business card with their Character Masks. This project highlights characters and descriptive language.

Materials:

Index cards	Hole punch
Pencil/pens/markers	Book ring
Business card samples	

Goals:

To create a business card for a story character
To describe a story character to someone else

Steps:

1. Look at different business cards to get an idea of how you want to design your card.
2. Punch a hole in the center of the left edge.
3. Draw a picture of the character, a logo, an address and the book title on the card front.
4. Write a character description on the back.
5. Use the book ring to fasten cards together.

Character Business Card Example

Logo

Picture

William

One Castle Drive
England

The Castle
In the attic
Book Title

Nick

Desription

William
Interesting
Little
Likeable
Intelligent
Awsome
Magical with
the coin

Real Estate Sales Brochure

The Real Estate Sales Brochure was recommended by the young authors in this book. They enjoyed presenting the setting through the perspective of a character they selected. This project highlights story setting and characters.

Materials:
8 1/2" x 11" paper   Pencil/pens/markers

Goals:
To create a sales brochure for property described in the story setting

To have a story character describe the setting as if he/she were a real estate salesperson

Steps:
1. Fold your paper into three columns.
2. Draw the character and write his/her name in column #1.
3. Draw a picture of the setting in column #2, 3, and 4. Describe it under the picture.
4. Write why the reader should buy this piece of property in column #5.
5. Write your name, the date, book title and author on column #6.

Real Estate Sales Brochure Example

Outside Page

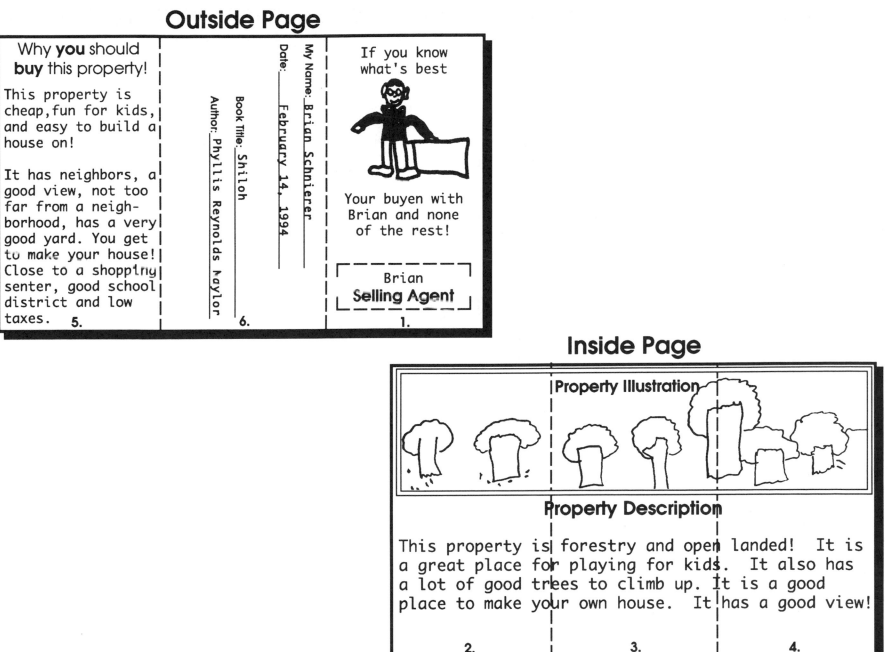

Why you should buy this property!

This property is cheap, fun for kids, and easy to build a house on!

It has neighbors, a good view, not too far from a neigh-borhood, has a very good yard. You get to make your house! Close to a shopping senter, good school district and low taxes. 5.

Book Title: Shiloh

Author: Phyllis Reynolds Naylor

6.

My Name: Brian Schnierer

Date: February 14, 1994

If you know what's best

Your buyen with Brian and none of the rest!

Brian
Selling Agent

1.

Inside Page

Property Illustration

Property Description

This property is forestry and open landed! It is a great place for playing for kids. It also has a lot of good trees to climb up. It is a good place to make your own house. It has a good view!

2.   3.   4.

3–Dimensional Project

The 3-Dimensional project was highly recommended by Julie Neupert's sixth-grade class. It highlights setting and characters.

Materials:

White paper (12" x 9")   Pencil/markers
Colored paper (11" x 9")   Stapler

Goal:

To create and display the characters from a story

Steps:

1. Select a scene from the story you would like to use for your project.
2. Measure and cut an 11" x 9" colored paper frame.
3. Create a strip of paper with the title and author of the book you are using.
4. Draw the setting on white 12" x 9" paper.
5. Draw your characters on a 11 1/2" x 9" sheet of paper. Make a 1" line for the characters to stand on at the bottom of the sheet.
6. Cut out the characters and 1" base.
7. Staple all three sheets together.

3-Dimensional Project Directions

Step 1

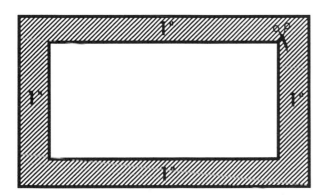

Measure and cut an 11" x 9" piece of colored construction paper.

Step 2

Hatchet by Gary Paulsen

Create a strip of paper and write the title and author of the book.

Step 3

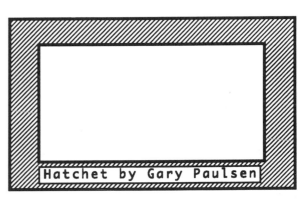

Glue the strip to the frame.

Step 4

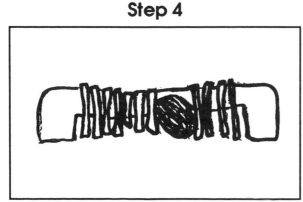

Draw the setting on white 12" x 9" paper.

Step 5 and Step 6

Draw your characters on a sheet of 11 1/2" x 9" paper. Make a 1" line for the characters to stand on at the bottom of the sheet. Cut them out.

Step 7

Staple the three sheets together.

Share your 3-D project with others.

T-Shirt Project

The Character T-Shirt was recommended by the third-grade students in Carol Fletcher's classroom. They enjoyed this project so much that they displayed their shirts on the walls. The Templeton t-shirt was designed by Brandon Alborg. This project can highlight characters and setting.

Materials:

T-shirt   Paint

Pencil   Paper

Goal:

To create a character t-shirt

Steps:

1. Select a plain t-shirt for your project.
2. Select a character for your t-shirt and draw it on white paper.
3. Using the paper drawing as a guide, draw the character on the t-shirt.
4. Draw over the design using fabric paint. Add any extra details and write the character's name on the shirt (see example).
5. Share and wear your special t-shirt.

T-Shirt Project Directions

Step 1

Select a plain t-shirt for your project.

Step 2

Select the character for your t-shirt and draw it on a piece of paper.

Step 3

Using the paper drawing as a guide, draw the character on your t-shirt.

Step 4

Draw over the design with fabric paint. Add any extra details you want. Write the character's name in paint somewhere on the shirt.

Step 5

TEMPLETON

Share and wear your special shirt.

ABC Book Project

The fourth graders in Valerie Marshall's and Martha Ivy's classroom recommend the ABC Book as a great project. They created a group book (see example) as they were reading books about the Oregon Trail. They integrated the vocabulary relevant to the time period into their book.

Materials:

White paper   Pencil/markers

Construction Paper (cover)

Goal:

To create an ABC book based on important language from a topic or time period

Steps:

1. Decide on the genre of your ABC book.
2. Read books of that genre (e.g. mystery).
3. Select a letter for your page. Re-read the books you have read looking for a word which starts with your letter and is important to the story.
4. Define the word on your page and draw a picture of it.
5. Select a person to illustrate the cover.
6. Gather all of the book pages and bind them together inside the cover.

ABC Book Sample Pages

(Allison Serano)

P is for Prairie Schooner Many Prairie Schooners traveled along the Oregon Trail carrying food and supplies so the pioneers could reach their destination.

(Kevi Louis-Johnson)

R is for rivers and rapids that many pioneers crossed such as the Platte, the Snake and the Columbia river.

(Blake Blair)

W is for walk. Most children walked beside covered wagons for the long Oregon trip.

(Travis Calhoun)

Y is for yoke. A yoke is something that is used to keep oxen together along the long trail to beautiful Oregon country.

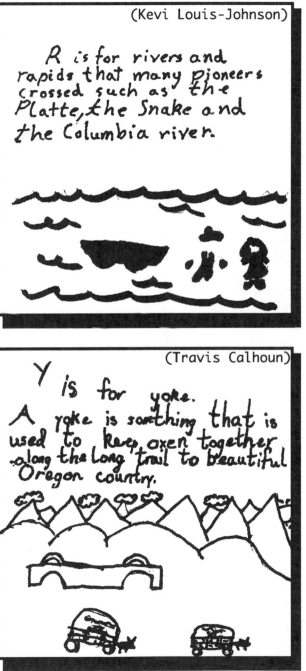

My Project Supply Sheet

Name:
My Project is: _____

To do my project I will need:

Writing Tools
___ pencil(s)
___ marker(s)
___ pen(s)
___ crayons
___
___
___

Art Supplies
___ glue
___ paste
___ scissors
___ paint
___ paint brush
___ glitter
___ stickers
___ tape
___ clay
___
___

Paper Supplies
___ form:page #
___ plain paper
___ lined paper
___ construction paper
___ cardstock paper
___ butcher paper
___ newspaper
___ cardboard
___ corrugated cardboard
___ contact paper
___ index card
___
___

Other Possible Items
___ book
___ shoe box
___ paper sack
___ t-shirt
___ yarn
___ cloth
___ string
___ business card samples
___ travel brochures
___ real estate brochures
___ book ring
___ hole punch
___ stapler

Chapter 7

Reference Books

Reference Books

Author	Book Title	Publisher
Atwell, Nancie	*Coming to Know*	Heinemann Educational Books, 1990
Calkins, Lucy McCormick	*The Art of Teaching Writing*	Heinemann Educational Books, 1986
Graves, Donald H.	*Writing: Teachers and Writers at Work*	Heinemann Educational Books, 1983
Johnson, Terry D. Louis, Daphne R.	*Literacy through Literature*	Heinemann Educational Books, 1987
Lukens, Rebecca J.	*A Critical Handbook of Children's Literature*	HarperCollins Publishers, 1990
Norton, Donna	*The Impact of Literature-Based Reading*	Macmillan Publishing Company, 1992
O'Brien-Palmer, Michelle	*Book-Write: A Creative Bookmaking Guide for Young Authors*	MicNik Publications, Inc., 1992
O'Brien-Palmer, Michelle	*Book-Talk: Exciting Literature Experiences for Kids*	MicNik Publications, Inc., 1993
Rothlein, Liz Meinbach, Anita Meyer	*The Literature Connection*	Scott, Foresman and Company, 1991

Chapter 8

Forms to Copy

"B.A.G. IT"
(Book Advice Guide)

Types of Books are "Genres"

- Fiction **F**
- Non–Fiction **NF**
- Mysteries ○
- Sports ○
- Realistic Fiction ○
- Adventure ○
- Biographies ○
- Fairytales and Folktales ○
- Historical Fiction ○
- Seasonal ○
- Poetry, Humor and Song ○

Level of Difficulty!!!

E Everybody

M Medium

C Challenge

 Forms from *Read and Write: Fun Literature and Writing Connections for Kids*, MicNik Publications, Inc.

Alluring Alliteration

Pattern Spider Pre-Write

Name:

Title:

 Forms from *Read and Write: Fun Literature and Writing Connections for Kids*, MicNik Publications, Inc.

Event Intensity Bar Graph

Name:

Title:

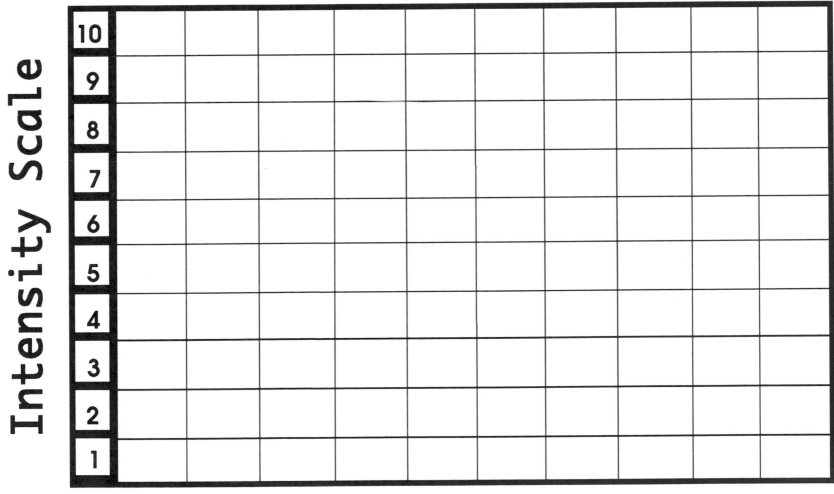

Intensity Scale

10
9
8
7
6
5
4
3
2
1

Story Events

Forms from *Read and Write: Fun Literature and Writing Connections for Kids*, MicNik Publications, Inc.

Style Tool Box

Name:

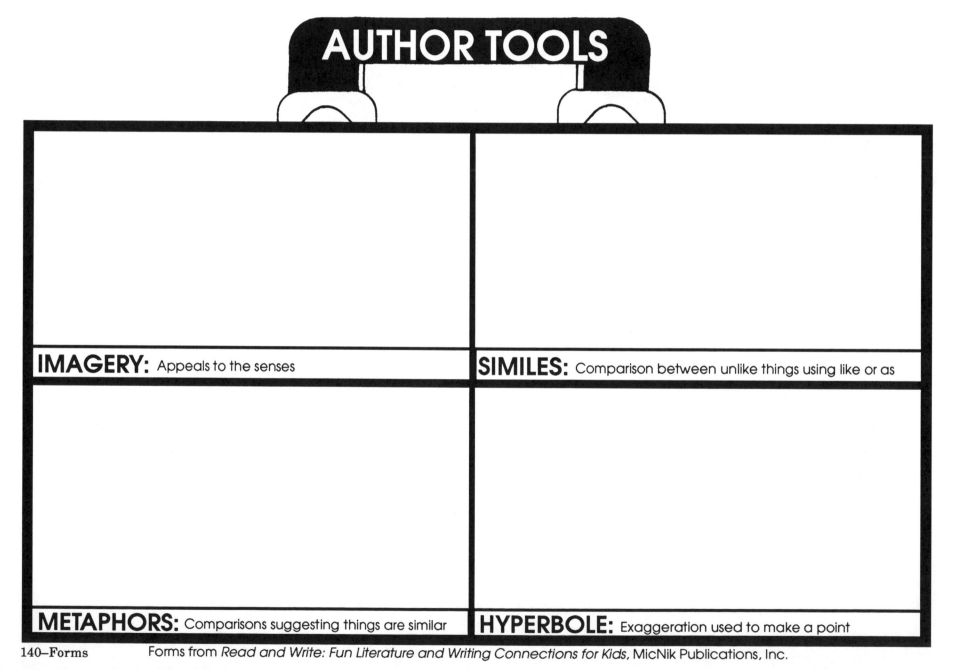

AUTHOR TOOLS

IMAGERY: Appeals to the senses

SIMILES: Comparison between unlike things using like or as

METAPHORS: Comparisons suggesting things are similar

HYPERBOLE: Exaggeration used to make a point

Forms from *Read and Write: Fun Literature and Writing Connections for Kids*, MicNik Publications, Inc.

Setting Stage

Name:
Title:
Author:

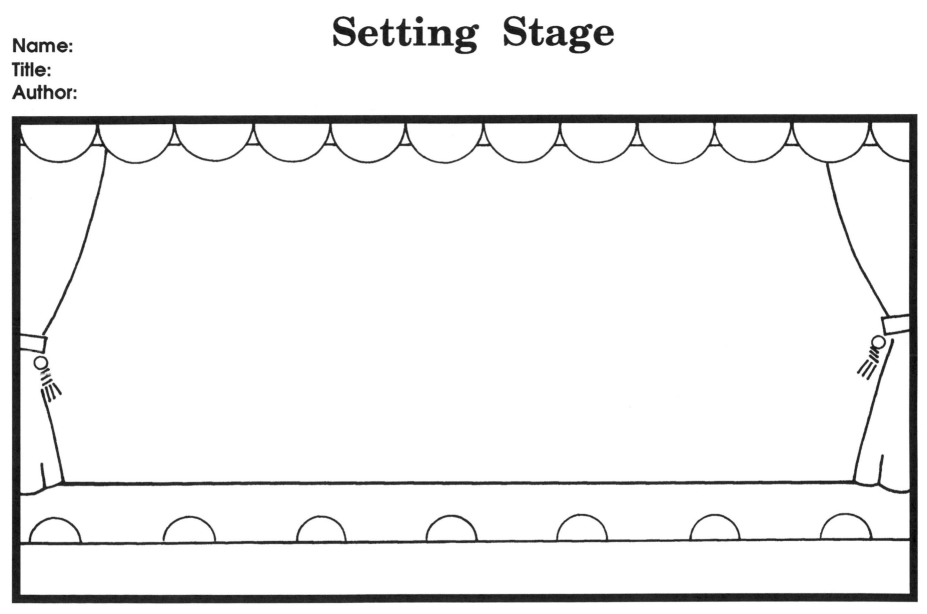

Description:

Setting Points

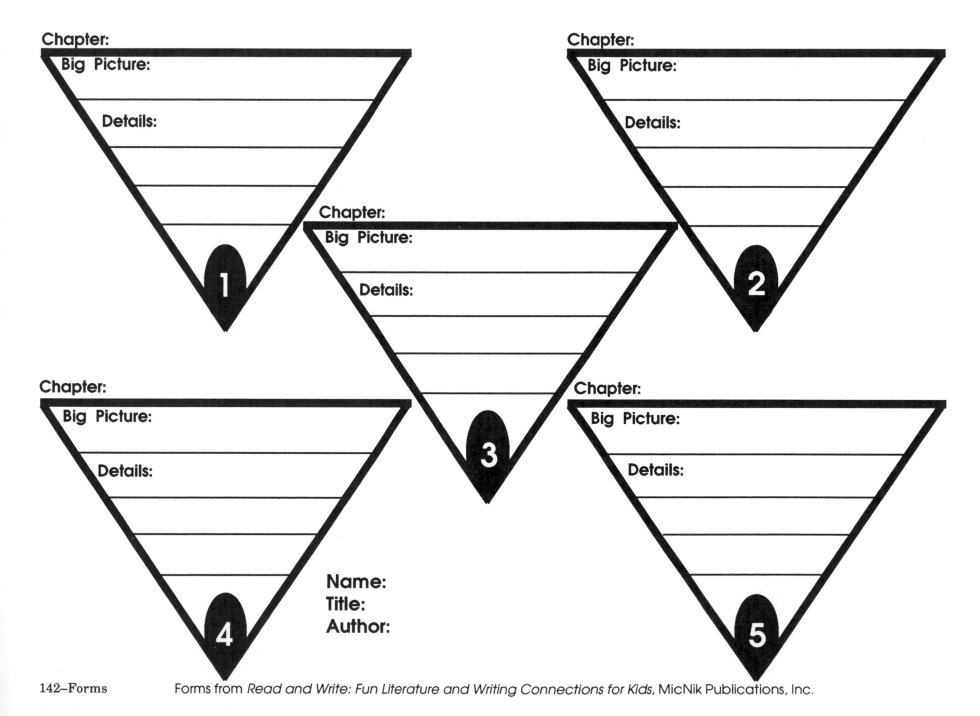

Chapter:
Big Picture:
Details:
1

Chapter:
Big Picture:
Details:
2

Chapter:
Big Picture:
Details:
3

Chapter:
Big Picture:
Details:
4

Chapter:
Big Picture:
Details:
5

Name:
Title:
Author:

 Forms from *Read and Write: Fun Literature and Writing Connections for Kids*, MicNik Publications, Inc.

Setting Check Sheet and Mood List

Name:

Title:

Author:

Possible Setting Moods

Tense ○
Mysterious ○
Humorous ○
Frightening ○
Gloomy ○
Thrilling ○
Serene ○
Intense ○
Hopeful ○
Exciting ○
Funny ○
Sad ○
Suspenseful ○
Happy ○
Unhappy ○
Scary ○
Silly ○
Lonely ○

1. How does the setting make you feel? Does it seem real to you? Yes ❑ No ❑
(Please explain on back)

2. Is it a place you would want to go? Yes❑ No❑
(Please explain on back)

3. The setting: _____ stays the same
_____ changes

Main Setting

Illustration

▶ **Place:** _____

_____

Time: _____

Mood: _____

_____

Time Capsule

Story Time Capsule for:

The story takes place:_____

The time period:_____

What it's like:_____

_____

_____

Timeline

Forms from *Read and Write: Fun Literature and Writing Connections for Kids*, MicNik Publications, Inc.

Setting Comparison

Name:

Title:

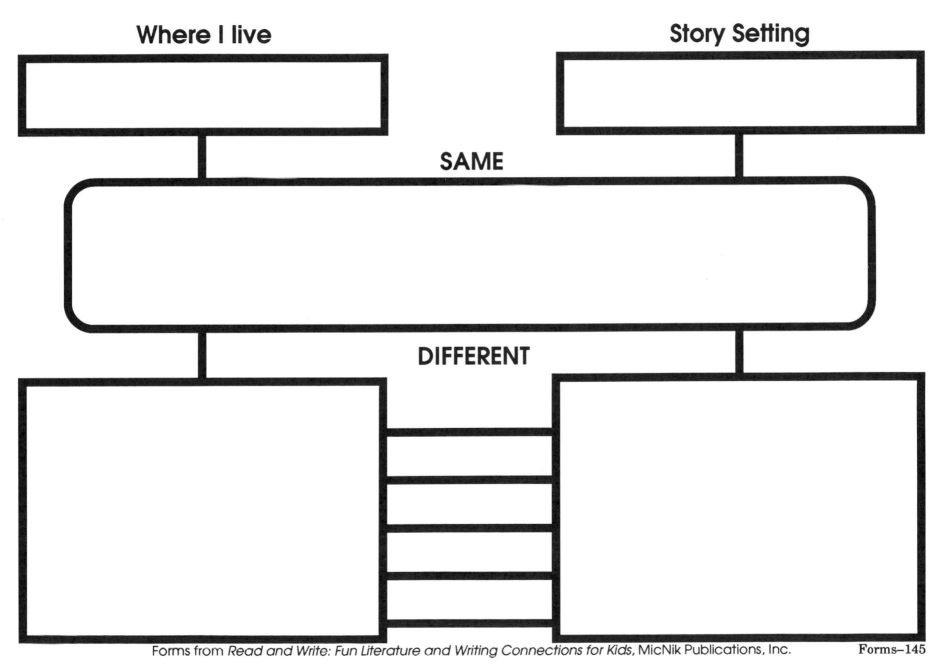

Where I live

Story Setting

SAME

DIFFERENT

Select–a–Setting

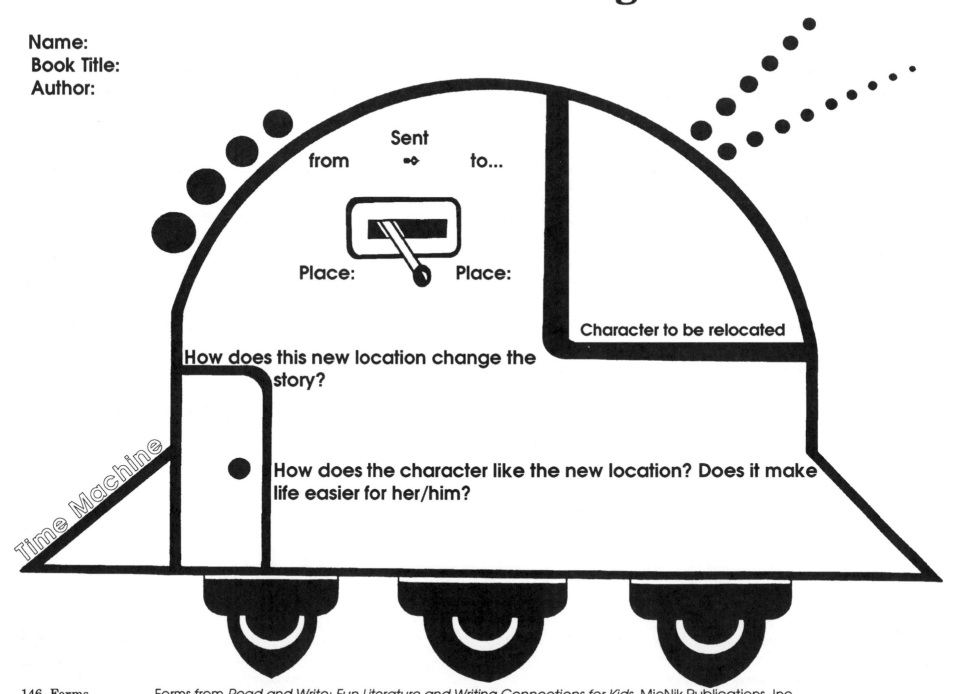

Name:
Book Title:
Author:

Sent

from ⊸ to...

Place: Place:

Character to be relocated

How does this new location change the story?

Time Machine

● How does the character like the new location? Does it make life easier for her/him?

Forms from *Read and Write: Fun Literature and Writing Connections for Kids*, MicNik Publications, Inc.

Character Scrapbook

Name:

Title:

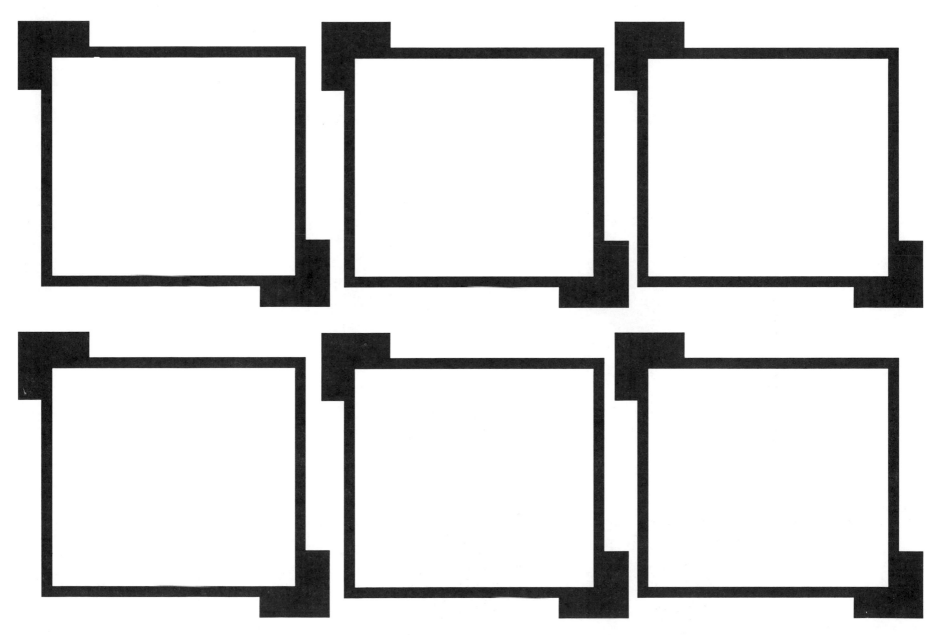

Sensational Sociogram

Name:

Title:

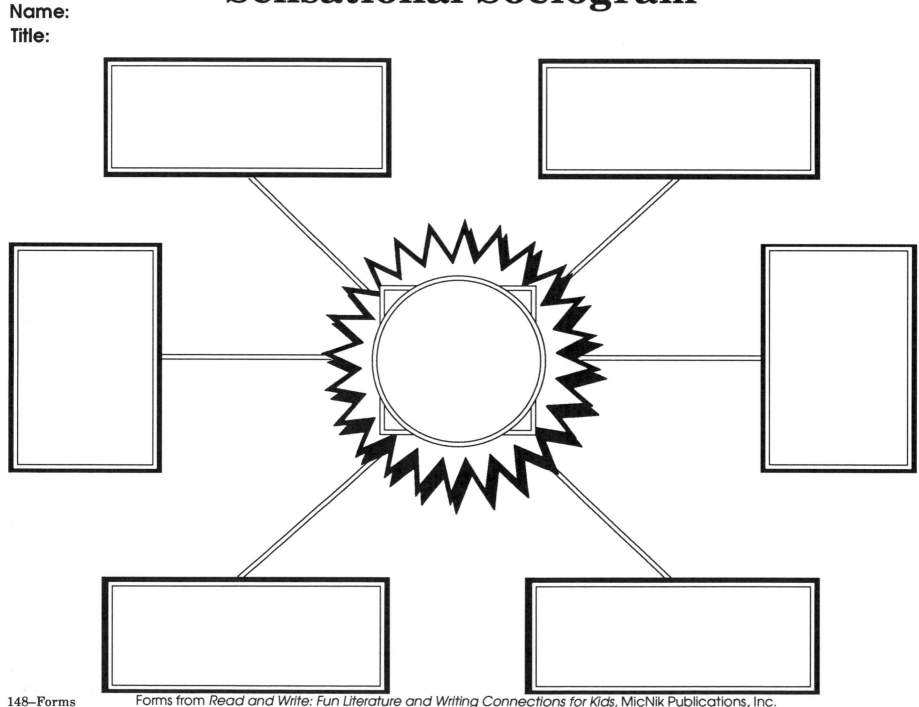

Forms from *Read and Write: Fun Literature and Writing Connections for Kids*, MicNik Publications, Inc.

Character Check Sheet and Traits List

Name:

Title:

1. Does the character seem real to you? Yes☐ No☐
   (Please explain on back)

2. Do the character's actions fit what you know
   of him/her? Yes☐ No☐ (Please explain on back)

3. This character is: _____ flat (stays the same)

   ◯ round (changes)

Common Character Traits

adventurous	friendly	pretty
awesome	fun-loving	quiet
artistic	gentle	rich
athletic	generous	respectful
active	happy	rad
beautiful	humble	sad
brave	hostile	sloppy
bold	honest	serious
bossy	intelligent	successful
cheerful	independent	shy
curious	Inventive	short
creative	leader	smart
courageous	lazy	studious
considerate	messy	selfish
daring	mischievious	simple
dreamer	mean	tall
dainty	neat	trustworthy
dangerous	nasty	thoughtful
exciting	nice	unselfish
entertaining	nosy	warm
energetic	open	witty
funny	poor	wild
fighter	proud	wonderful

Character Traits ▶

_____

_____

_____

_____

_____

Illustration

Character Profile

Character Name:

Book Title:

Interests

Personal Information

Age ____

Boy	❑
Girl	❑
Man	❑
Woman	❑
Other	❑

Hair Color

Black	❑
Blonde	❑
Brown	❑
Red	❑
Grey	❑
White	❑

Eye Color

Black	❑
Blue	❑
Brown	❑
Green	❑
Pink	❑

Weight

Thin	❑
Average	❑
Heavy	❑

Height

Short	❑
Average	❑
Tall	❑

Personality/Interests

Scale

	not 1	2	3	4	very 5
Adventurous	❑	❑	❑	❑	❑
Courageous	❑	❑	❑	❑	❑
Flexible	❑	❑	❑	❑	❑
Friendly	❑	❑	❑	❑	❑
Happy	❑	❑	❑	❑	❑
Helpful	❑	❑	❑	❑	❑
Kind	❑	❑	❑	❑	❑
Organized	❑	❑	❑	❑	❑
Patient	❑	❑	❑	❑	❑
Responsible	❑	❑	❑	❑	❑
Smart	❑	❑	❑	❑	❑
Trustworthy	❑	❑	❑	❑	❑
Other: _____	❑	❑	❑	❑	❑

Where character lives:

Favorites

Color_____

Number _____

Sport _____

Game _____

Hobby _____

Food _____

Music _____

Animal_____

Subject _____

Friend _____

Other:

Profile by:_____

Forms from *Read and Write: Fun Literature and Writing Connections for Kids*, MicNik Publications, Inc.

Character Map

Name:

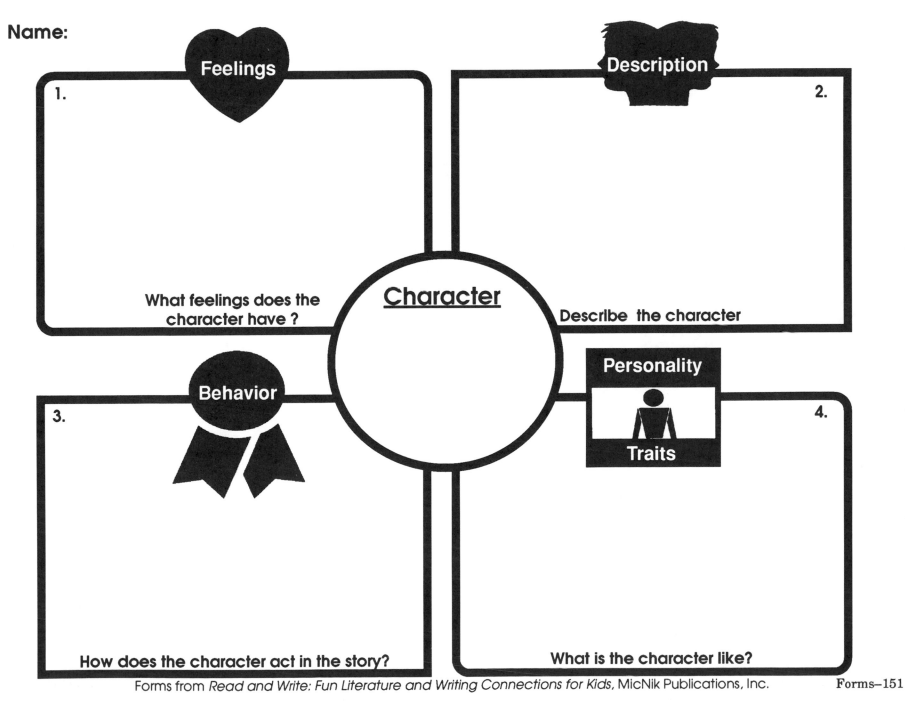

Feelings

1.

What feelings does the character have ?

Description

2.

Describe the character

Character

Behavior

3.

How does the character act in the story?

Personality

Traits

4.

What is the character like?

Char-a-Graph

Name:

Character:

Title:

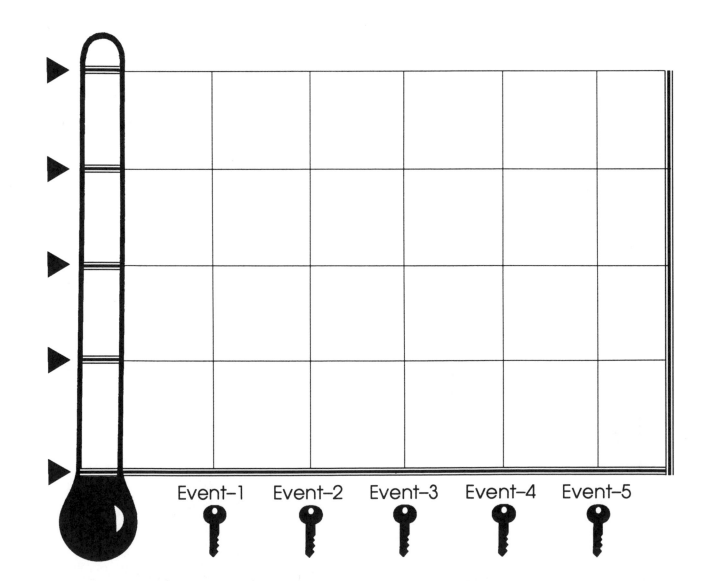

Character Trait Scale

Event-1   Event-2   Event-3   Event-4   Event-5

Filmstrip Story Sequencer

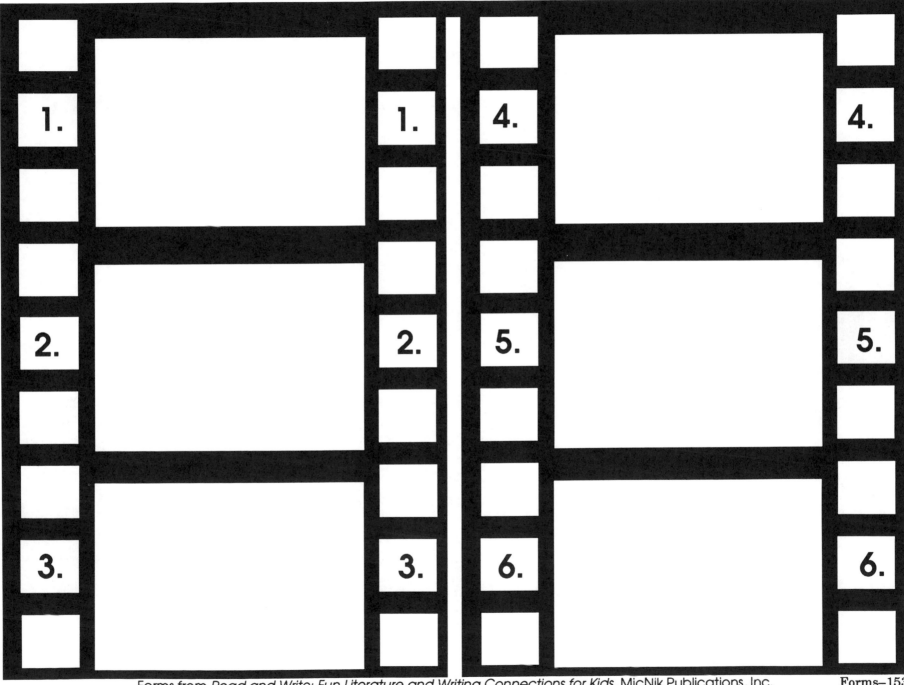

Story Train

Name:

Title:

What happened first? What happened next? What happened last?

Beginning　　　　Middle　　　　End

Description:

 Forms from *Read and Write: Fun Literature and Writing Connections for Kids*, MicNik Publications, Inc.

Story Map

Name:

Title:

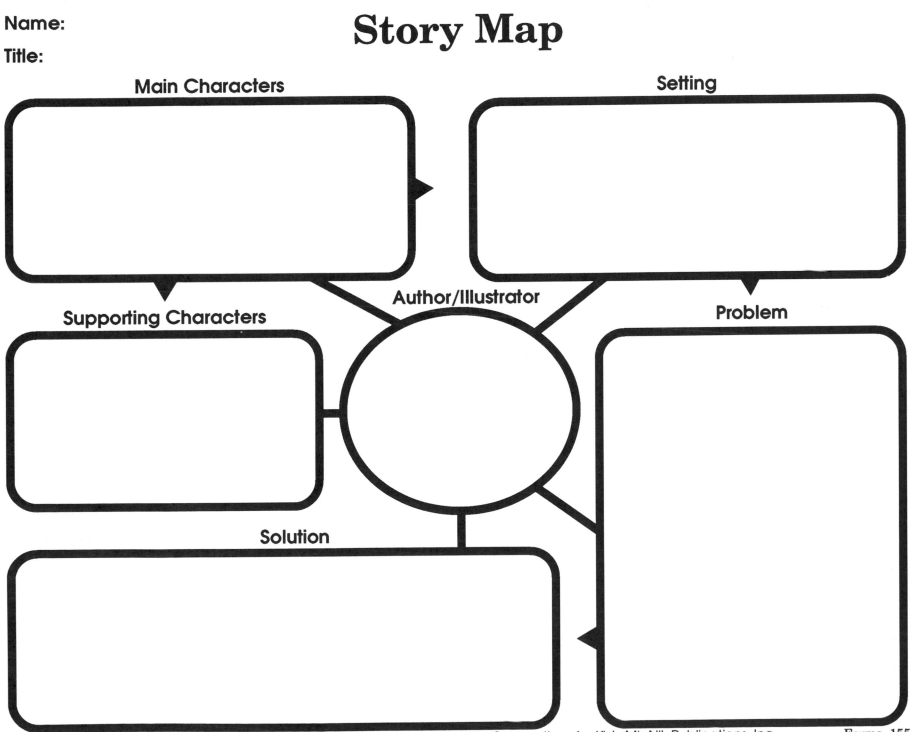

Main Characters

Setting

Supporting Characters

Author/Illustrator

Problem

Solution

Forms from *Read and Write: Fun Literature and Writing Connections for Kids*, MicNlk Publications, Inc.

Problem & Solution Diagram

Name:

Book Title:

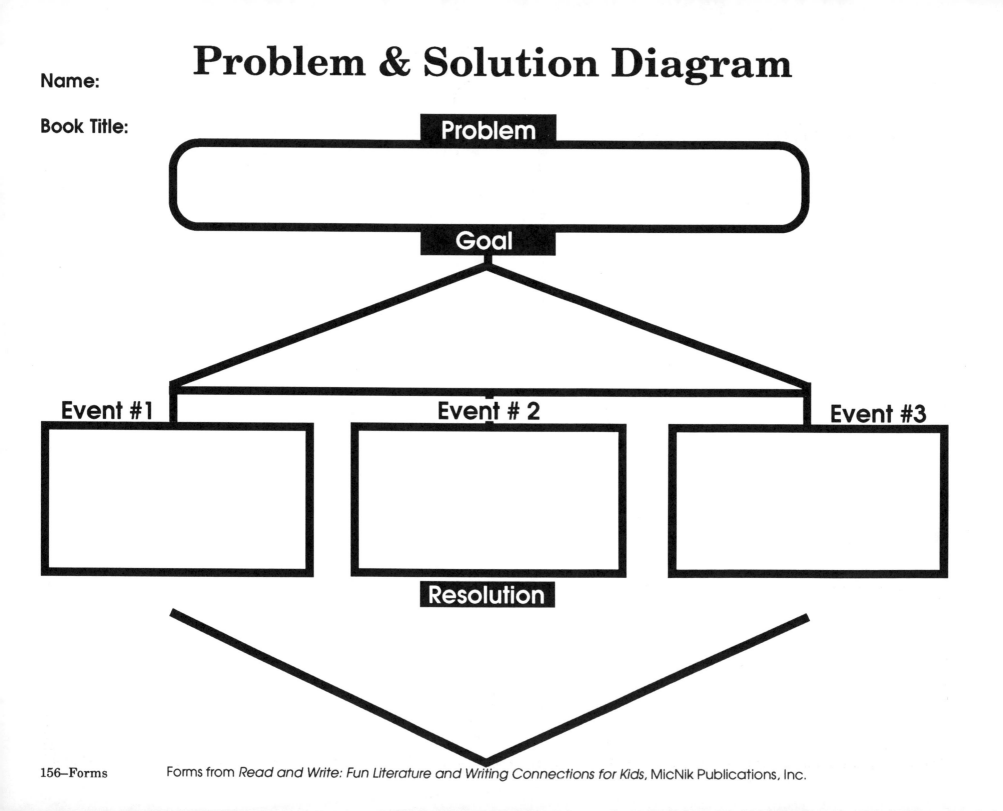

Problem

Goal

Event #1

Event # 2

Event #3

Resolution

 Forms from *Read and Write: Fun Literature and Writing Connections for Kids*, MicNik Publications, Inc.

Plot Check Sheet and Conflict List

Name:

Title:

1. Did you feel like you were part of the story? Yes☐ No☐
   (Please explain on back)

2. Were you able to guess what was going to happen at the end ? Yes☐ No☐ (Please explain on back)

3. What do you think was the best part of the story?

Conflict List

Check one or more

Character vs. Nature ☐
Character vs. Self ☐
Character vs. Society ☐
Character vs. Character ☐

Main Problem ▶ _____

_____

Character's Goal ▶ _____

_____

Resolution ▶ _____

Graph-a-Plot

Name:
Title:

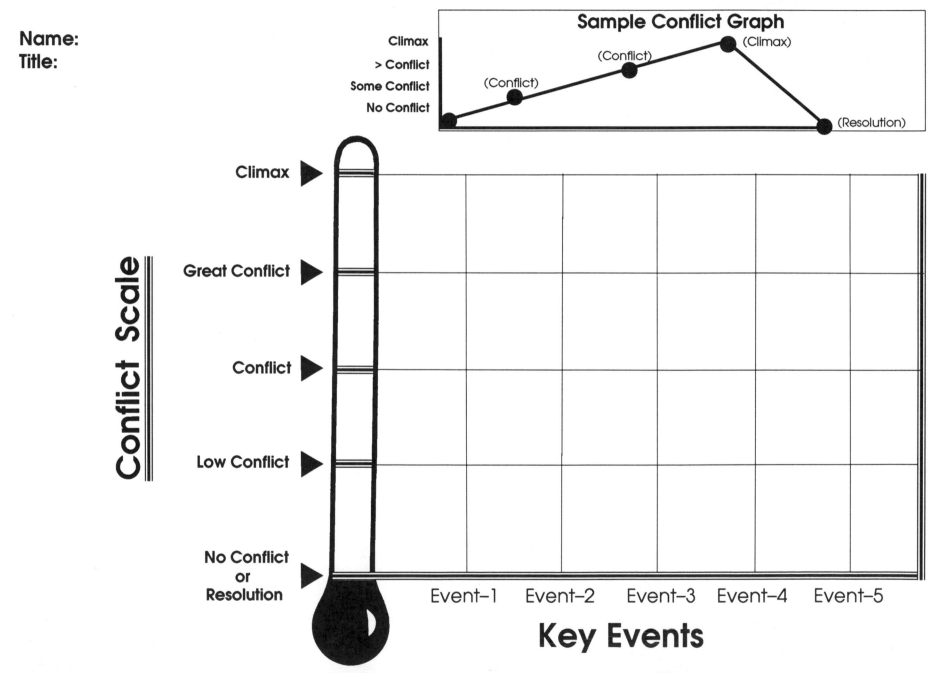

Sample Conflict Graph

Climax
> Conflict
Some Conflict
No Conflict

(Conflict)
(Conflict)
(Climax)
(Resolution)

Conflict Scale

Climax ▶
Great Conflict ▶
Conflict ▶
Low Conflict ▶
No Conflict
or
Resolution ▶

Event–1   Event–2   Event–3   Event–4   Event–5

Key Events

Forms from *Read and Write: Fun Literature and Writing Connections for Kids*, MicNik Publications, Inc.

ABOUT THE AUTHOR
Of...

READ & WRITE
BOOK-TALK
BOOK-WRITE
THROUGH MY EYES
BOOK-TALK CASSETTE

Michelle received her undergraduate and graduate degrees at the University of Washington. Michelle is 39 years old and lives in the Pacific Northwest with her son and husband. She is an educational consultant and speaker. Michelle always includes children in the creation of her books and tapes.

WORKSHOPS AND ASSEMBLIES
for more information, please call (206) 881-6476 or write to
MicNik Publications, Inc. • P.O. Box 3041 • Kirkland, WA 98083

WORKSHOPS FOR TEACHERS
Book-Talk and Book-Write

Presented by...
Michelle O'Brien-Palmer

Practical ideas from real classrooms:

Book-Talk
- *Bringing literature into your classroom*
- *Starting your own literature circles*
- *Prediction, retelling, and reviewing strategies*
- *Reading projects recommended by kids*

Book-Write
- *The 5-Step Writing Process in action*
- *Setting, character, and plot development*
- *Great bookmaking ideas*
- *Journal starters and fun writing projects*

WORKSHOPS FOR KIDS
Read & Write

Presented by...
Michelle O'Brien-Palmer

Interactive Workshops for K-6th*

can include...
- 5-Step Writing Process
- Genre – book selection
- Story elements
- Character developement
- Setting development
- Plot development
- Book-making
- Fun projects

Workshops are tailored to the needs of each classroom.

ASSEMBLIES FOR SCHOOLS
Book-Talk and Book-Write

Featuring:

Michelle O'Brien-Palmer	*Author*
Heidi Stephens	*Illustrator*
Nancy Stewart	*Musician*

Drop Everything and Read!
A musical celebration of books and readers. Selections include; I Love the Library, Genre Tree, Hello Fiction, Remarkable Reviewers, and many more.

I'm An Author and So Are You!
A musical celebration of young authors and writing. Selections include; Just 5-Steps, Make a Book, Every Story Has..., I Want to Be An Illustrator, and many more.

MicNik Publications, Inc.

Book-Talk does for reading what *Book-Write* does for writing. It is a fun, clear, easy-to-follow resource guide for teachers and parents who want to encourage a lifelong love of literature. *Book-Talk* is filled with real kids' examples and reproducible forms.

11" x 8 1/2" • 160 pages • $16.95
ISBN 1-879235-02-1

A fun, easy-to-follow, bookmaking guide for young authors. Filled with examples of other young authors' books. A wonderful resource for teachers and parents interested in the writing process. Reproducible forms for use in the classroom or at home.

11" x 8 1/2" • 128 pages • $16.95
ISBN 1-879235-01-3

A look at life through the eyes of a young child. Co-authored and illustrated by children – the poetry in *Through My Eyes* has brought joy to readers all over the country. There is space for young authors to write their own poems in the back of this book.

5 1/2" x 8 1/2" • 33 pages • $6.95
ISBN 1-879235-00-5

BOOK-TALK (Cassette)
Singable Songs for Lifelong Readers

Combining music, learning and fun, this tape captures the essence of literature for young readers (K-4th). Starting with an inspiring and unforgettable tune called *Drop Everything and Read*, BOOK-TALK is a musical celebration of literature and readers. Alone, or as a companion to the book, this tape is an excellent resource for classrooms and home.

$9.95, ISBN 1-879235-03-X

A great resource guide which invites children (K-6th), teachers and parents to explore and experience the dynamic connections between reading and writing. The young authors blossom as they link the books they are reading to their own wriitng. Fun projects recommended by kids and reproducible forms are included. Great for home and school.

11" x 8 1/2" • 160 pages • $16.95
ISBN 1-879235-04-8